THE SOUTHERN SUDAN

The Southern Sudan

From Conflict to Peace

by MOHAMED OMER BESHIR

BOOKS
10 East 53d St., New York 10022
(a division of Harper & Row Publishers, Inc.)

First published in the United Kingdom by
C. Hurst & Co. (Publishers) Ltd., London

© 1975 by Mohamed Omer Beshir

Printed in Great Britain

Published in the U.S.A. 1975 by
Harper & Row Publishers, Inc.
Barnes & Noble Import Division

ISBN: 0-06-490379-6

CONTENTS

Page

INTRODUCTION ix

Chapters

I. From the Round Table Conference to the Twelve-Man Committee 1

II. Political Developments and the Southern Question 1965–1969 24

III. Origin and Development of Southern Political Organisations 45

IV. The May Revolution and the Southern Problem 72

V. Steps leading to the Addis Ababa Agreement 99

VI. Conclusion 122

APPENDICES

A. Policy Statement of the Southern Question by President Nimeiri, 9 June 1969 155

B. The Addis Ababa Agreement on the Problem of South Sudan: Draft Organic Law to organise Regional Self-Government in the Provinces of the Democratic Republic of Sudan 158

INDEX 178

MAPS

1. Democratic Republic of the Sudan vi
2. Southern Sudan: Principal Tribes vii

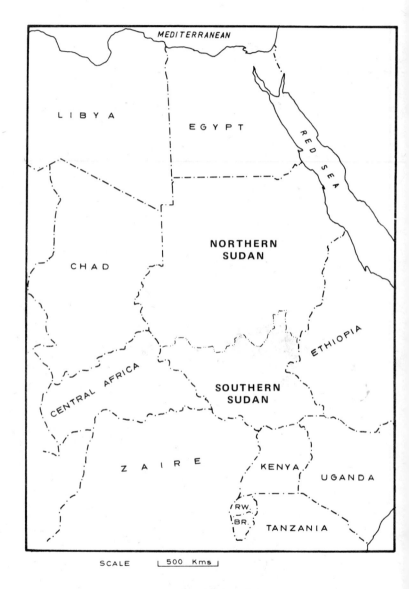

MEDITERRANEAN

LIBYA

EGYPT

RED SEA

NORTHERN
SUDAN

CHAD

CENTRAL AFRICA

SOUTHERN
SUDAN

ETHIOPIA

ZAIRE

KENYA

UGANDA

RW.

BR.

TANZANIA

SCALE   500 Kms

1. Democratic Republic of the Sudan

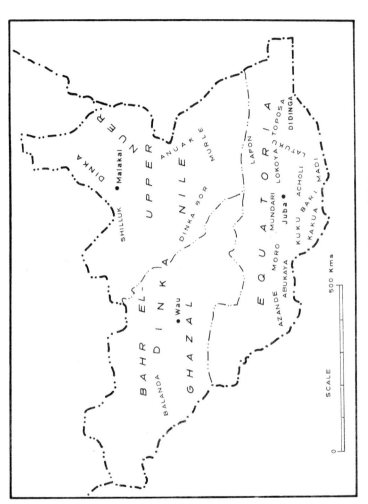

2. Southern Sudan: Principal Tribes

INTRODUCTION

This book is about the search for peace in the Southern Sudan — how it came and how it has been achieved. It is about the way the conflict between the North and the South has been resolved. In my first book, *The Southern Sudan: Background to Conflict,* I dealt with the rise of the problem of the Southern Sudan and how it was perpetuated over the years. I also dealt with the roots of the problem in their perspectives, both geographical and historical, and with how the British policy during the Condominium administration had contributed to the conflict. In the concluding chapter of that book I wrote as follows: —

> The immediate task . . . is to achieve peace in the South while keeping open the dialogue between the North and the South. The peace offensive must be pursued on all fronts, for which every possible resource must be mobilised, and help enlisted from all who are keen to see peace return to the South and national unity built in the Sudan.

The first part of this plea has been fulfilled, and this book is about what followed after the Round Table Conference and about the search for peace which finally culminated in the Addis Ababa Agreement of 1972. The special, secret minute agreed to at the Round Table Conference, which has not been published before, is included. It was hoped to include the full record of the Round Table Conference and of the Twelve-Man Committee, but this has not been possible for reasons of space.

An attempt is made to survey and describe the rise of the Anya-Nya and its organisation, and the South Sudan Liberation Movement. The concluding chapter deals with the problem of national unity in the Sudan, and suggests certain lines of approach and action.

Problems of conflict within nations and problems of

nation-building are not peculiar to the Sudan. There have been few societies on any continent which have been free from national or community conflict of one sort or another. Even countries which have been assumed to have achieved national integration, such as Britain, Canada and Belgium, are found today to be facing the problem. Nigeria, Burundi, India, Pakistan, Ceylon, Malaysia and Lebanon, are examples of countries in the developing world facing the problems of conflict and nation-building.

National reconciliation might have been achieved for the present time in the Sudan, but in order to make this a permanent feature, the Sudanese, both in the North and in the South, need to continuously review their policies and achievements both internally and externally. Although confidence has been rapidly restored, a great deal needs to be done before stability and progress are achieved.

Francis Mading Deng, in his book *Dynamics of Identification* (Khartoum University Press, 1974, p. 102) writes:

> Although regional self-rule is a short-term solution to the South-North problems, it is hard to expect that the Southern Sudanese will be content with regional participation and not concerned with such major national and international issues as what Sudan's identification should be.

He goes on (p. 109):

> The issue for the Sudan, it would seem, is finding out and formulating those symbols which would tend to unite rather than divide without threatening participants whose support is pivotal to stability. With these symbols to guide development, with autonomy to ensure the security of those whose support is vital, with full interaction between the various parts of the country, and with calculated action at all levels to maximise the net outcomes, there is reason to believe that there could emerge a genuine consciousness of the wider Sudan as a basis for a common national identification and unification.

The *Progress Report of the Provisional High Executive Council* for the period April 1972 to October 1973 shows how difficult these tasks are. It states (p. 17): 'The task ahead is vast and will need money, material resources and manpower, beyond what the country alone can provide.' The achievements during the year following the Addis Ababa Agreement recorded in the Report are impressive, but the problems and difficulties are also many. Exposure to modern influences does not necessarily lead to the disappearance of conflict. On the contrary, it might create the conditions for the eruption of conflicts which impede the process of integration.

The future will depend on how objectively, seriously and intelligently the problems of change are handled. In this exercise, communication between the Northerners and Southerners, at all levels, especially that of the policy- and decision-makers, is important. Failure to communicate in the past has been one of the reasons for conflict. The aim of this book, like that of the previous one, is to contribute to better knowledge and understanding, and to stimulate discussion and communication.

In writing this book, I have relied in the first place on my own experiences and personal information, but I also drew on information and experiences of many friends, in both the North and the South, who shared with me the same interest and concern. Other friends, who prefer to remain unnamed, provided me with information which would not otherwise have been easily available. They encouraged me to write this book as a sequel to the first one, hoping that this would help in the promotion of confidence and in the construction of the future. Any mistakes or wrong judgments are my own responsibility.

Khartoum, 25 May 1974 M.O.B.

CHAPTER I

FROM THE ROUND TABLE CONFERENCE TO THE TWELVE-MAN COMMITTEE

The story of the Round Table Conference, how it was convened and its conclusions, has been told in *The Southern Sudan: Background to Conflict.*[1] Since then there have been a number of writings by Northern and Southern Sudanese reflecting on the Round Table Conference.[2] Some have suggested that it failed in its objectives: the fact that it did not reach a decision on the status of the Southern Sudan at that time and that hostilities continued in the months that followed was looked upon as proof of that failure. Foreign correspondents dismissed the Conference as another example of the futility of looking for unity and peace between the North and the South through discussions and conferences. Churchmen and missionaries, who had always felt justified in making pronouncements on the origins and reasons for the conflict, dismissed the Conference as a failure.

Those Africans of other states who had followed the events in the Sudan were disappointed. People in both the North and the South with extreme views wrote the Conference off and began to advocate a military solution, something which they had stood against in the past and for which they had condemned the military regime of General Ibrahim Abboud. A Southerner, writing later, summed up his views on the Conference as follows:

> Subsequent events, however, showed that the Arabs had only tried to test Southern negotiating ability, gain time and Northern public opinion, and use all the excuses there are in the world to solve the problem in their own way.

Although the Southern delegates were perfectly aware of this, the Conference Hall did not present fertile ground for the expression of suspicions and they had to look as though they accepted each other's promises![3]

However, as subsequent events were to prove, these critics and pessimists were wrong; they had failed to see the Conference in the context of the origins and development of the problem, the struggle for political power at the time between the different groups in the North, and the divisions and disagreements among the Southern political groups inside and outside the Sudan. From the beginning, there had been many problems, organizational, political and other. To have overcome these problems and held the Conference at all was the true success.

The first problem had related to the organizational side of the Conference. Once the proposal made by William Deng, then President of the Sudan African National Union (S.A.N.U.), to hold a conference was agreed to by the transitional government of Sir Al Khatim Al Khalifa in January 1965, the first questions which arose were — 'How should the conference be organised?' and 'Who should organise it?' Although the majority of political parties were represented in the Cabinet there were a few political groups from the North and the South which remained outside the Government. The composition of the Cabinet itself did not reflect the real political weight of the political parties, and this was a source of continuous tension and conflict within it. The Cabinet was so busy with the dismantling of the military régime and the clearing-up operations, that it had little time to devote to the problem. Quick action, not to be hampered by political conflicts and by red tape, was needed if the conference was to be held at all. S.A.N.U. did not trust the Northern political parties and they in turn did not trust S.A.N.U., which to them was an unknown quantity. Hence there was the need for a body that would undertake the work of the conference and which, while enjoying the confidence of the different political parties and S.A.N.U., would also be trusted by the Cabinet and work under its guidance.

I was approached by Dawood Abdel Latif at the end of January 1965, just after he had come back from Kampala and after the Prime Minister's announcement that the

Government had agreed to hold the conference, to be the General Secretary of the conference. I agreed on the condition that the Cabinet would bless my selection, and that I would have the freedom to select those who would join the secretariat. The Prime Minister later confirmed that the Cabinet had agreed to both these points and informed me that he would give his personal and official support for the organisation of the conference. I was informed that the secretariat would be an impartial independent body working with both political parties and the Cabinet through a liaison officer – a job undertaken by Hassan Ahmed Yousif, who was the Prime Minister's personal assistant at the time.

Work on the formation of the secretariat and finding the appropriate offices for our work was immediately started. A list of those whom I knew personally and trusted to dedicate themselves to the success of the conference was drawn up. I was less concerned with the political parties to which each belonged than with their ability to organise, prepare documents, undertake public relations and, if need be, persuade and negotiate.

The first to join the secretariat was Mahjoub Mohamed Salih, then editor of *Al Ayam* Newspaper, Abdel Aziz Al Nasri, then Counsellor in the Ministry of Foreign Affairs, Yousif Mohamed Ali of the Attorney General's Department, who later became Chairman of the Twelve-Man Committee, and Abdel Rahman Abdulla of the Institute of Public Administration, who was later one of those who participated in the Addis Ababa Agreement. Mohamed Ibrahim Abu Salim, the Sudan Government archivist, Osman Sid Ahmed Ismail and Mudathir Abdel Rahim both of the University of Khartoum, were made responsible for documentation.

It was necessary from the beginning to ensure that the secretariat would include Southern Sudanese. Darius Beshir, who had helped Dawood Abdel Latif on his difficult mission to Kampala, became a member of the secretariat. Philip Obang, who had then just returned from abroad where he was training for ministry in the Church, was also invited to join us. Abel Alier, who was then in the Judiciary, was approached and he agreed to work with us on the secretariat, but the Chief Justice refused to release him.

The formation of the secretariat in this way overcame the

first problem and removed some of the doubts about the organizational aspects of the conference.

The second problem related to the implementation of the agreement reached by Dawood Abdel Latif and Darius Beshir in Kampala. On their return to Khartoum, and after discussion with the Cabinet, it became clear that some of the conditions agreed to by S.A.N.U. could not be fulfilled. First there was the state of emergency. S.A.N.U. had made its lifting throughout the Southern Sudan a condition for attending the conference. Although S.A.N.U. had appealed to the Southern Sudanese to call off the fighting, there was little response. On the contrary, there were signs of more tension between the Southerners and Northerners in the three main towns of the South: Juba, Wau and Malakal.

Rumours were circulating in Khartoum that the Anya Nya were marching through the streets of Juba and Wau. It was reported that Northern merchants and traders were considering closing down their businesses in the different parts of the South. Reports were also received that the inhabitants of Maridi were evacuating the town in fear of the Anya Nya.

These reports were exaggerated but not totally untrue. The amnesty declared by the Government on 10 December 1964 had encouraged the Anya Nya to come out of the forest. In some cases they threatened the merchants and defied the soldiers who were given orders not to shoot except in self-defence. Large numbers of Southerners left for the South after the December 1964 events in Khartoum when there were serious clashes between Northerners and Southerners and many Southerners lost their lives in these clashes. The returning Southerners went either on their own initiative, or with the encouragement of the Ministry of the Interior, who gave them full Government travel warrants. The tales they told on arrival added to the panic which already existed there. The Minister of the Interior was criticized for his action and even accused by the press of being party to what was taking place in the South.

On the other hand, the group of Southern politicians living outside the Sudan, who did not agree to the negotiations and were opposed to the leadership of William Deng, sent their own emissaries to the three Southern provinces to persuade their supporters not to lay down their arms or agree to the conference. This created confusion, which was increased by the activities of the Southern Front.

The Southern Front, which came into being only after October 1964 and chose to be active inside the Sudan, needed to establish itself and gain support before a conference could be held. It was afraid that given the disunity among the Southern political leadership outside the Sudan, the conference would be to the advantage of the North rather than to the South. As a result of all this, there was little response to S.A.N.U.'s appeals, and the Government was unable to lift the state of emergency.

Secondly, there was the issue of the venue for the Conference. Juba had been agreed to for this purpose, and it was further agreed that the state of emergency in Juba town would be lifted for the purpose of the negotiations. Again it was clear that this condition could not be met by the Government. The Northern political parties indicated their unwillingness to attend a conference in Juba if the state of emergency were lifted. S.A.N.U. and the Southern Front, while agreeing that the state of emergency in the whole South could not be lifted, insisted on holding the conference in Juba and at least on lifting the state of emergency in the town.

The secretariat needed to be satisfied that conditions in Juba were such that it was impossible to hold the Conference there. Two members of the secretariat flew there in February and on their return reported unfavourably on the situation. I travelled to Juba and held meetings with those responsible for the administration and security; all advised that Juba was unsuitable at that time for holding the Conference for security reasons. They informed me that feelings were running high and tension between Northerners and Southerners was growing. Northern merchants and officials were outspoken in their opposition to the Conference and negotiations.

When I went round the town I was struck by the display of military cars and when I asked about these I was told that this was connected with the lifting of arms to the Congo. The transitional Government's new line in foreign policy and its declarations of active support for revolutionary movements in Africa invited the hostility of both the Congo and Ethiopia. The co-operation of United States and Belgian forces with Tshombe had been publicly condemned. Demonstrators had attacked the U.S. embassy, and the Government called on the Security Council to discuss the 'imperialist aggression' and on the Organization of African Unity for action. By the beginning of the year, Algerian and Egyptian arms were being sent through Khartoum across the South to the Congolese rebels. I came to the conclusion that Juba did not provide a favourable climate for the negotiations and the ultimate success of the Conference. In particular, it would not be in the interests of the Sudan's relations with its neighbours: foreign observers and journalists would see in daylight the military activities in support of the Congolese rebels, which would have compromised rather than served the cause of Sudanese unity. My own conclusions were that there were serious security problems in Juba and this was reported back to the Prime Minister and the Cabinet.

It was difficult to persuade the Southern political parties to change the venue of the Conference, but they finally agreed to hold it in Khartoum. Thus the second problem was overcome.

Thirdly, there was the problem of the observers to be invited and of who was to chair the meetings. The agreement signed by the Sudan Government and Uganda in December 1964 had provided for the establishment of an observer team to supervise the return of refugees to the Sudan. It was envisaged that this team would be made up of nationals of the same countries that were members of the Commission for Refugees established by the O.A.U. in its meeting on 7 December 1964, namely Cameroon, Ghana, the Sudan, Tanzania and Uganda. Thus when the proposal for an observer team was made, the Sudanese Government accepted it in principle. When the agreement was later signed with S.A.N.U. in January 1965, the question of observers was accepted in the same spirit, and it was agreed to invite the Uganda Government to send an observer to the negotiations. The Northern political parties, while agreeing to all this, proposed that the number of observers should be enlarged but did not suggest a criterion for the selection of countries to be invited to send them. The Southern Front, which until then represented S.A.N.U. in the preliminary preparation inside the Sudan, did not object but suggested that only countries harbouring Sudanese refugees should be invited, together with a representative of the O.A.U. to represent the whole of Africa. It was also suggested that the United Nations be invited to send an observer.

The Northern political parties objected to both the O.A.U. and the U.N. for fear of internationalising the problem, which to them was an internal one. They argued that if it was necessary to invite observers they should be from among the Sudan's neighbours in the first place. They suggested the inclusion of Egypt because of its close historical associations with the Sudan and its interest in the Nile waters, and of Nigeria because of its similar problems. Algeria and Ghana were proposed because they were looked upon as the progressive African countries dedicated to the concepts of unity, Pan-Africanism and anti-imperialism. They argued that Ethiopia and Congo be excluded because both were involved in helping the rebels in the South. After a great deal of discussion, it was finally agreed to invite observers from Uganda, Kenya, Nigeria, Egypt, Ghana, Tanzania and Algeria. This satisfied the original Southern proposal to have outside observers, but because of the careful selection of the countries, it did not represent to the Northern political parties an internationalisation of the problem which they had feared.

Subsequent events proved how valuable and constructive the observers were. They took part not only in the public sessions of the Conference but also in the negotiations outside it. The representatives — especially those of Uganda, Ghana, Nigeria and Algeria — were active and instilled the feeling in the delegates that the Conference should never be allowed to fail. They advocated the need to unite, to shake off the imperialist inheritances and conciliate religious differences.

As for the issue of who was to chair the meeting, the Southern political parties argued that since the Secretary-General was from the North, the chairman should be chosen by the Southerners, and he could be from the North or the South. Again, it was difficult to agree on the criteria by which his impartiality could be established. Furthermore, it was important to find a man who could co-operate with the secretariat and take part, if necessary, in the delicate negotiations before and after the Conference without losing – or being seen to lose – his impartiality. The names of Babiker Awadalla, the Chief Justice, and Abdel Mageed Imam, a judge of the Supreme Court, were suggested among others, but not accepted.

Finally it was agreed to appoint the Vice-Chancellor of the University of Khartoum on the grounds that the University is an independent institution and had played a significant part in the October Revolution: the discussions held in the University on the Southern problem had sparked it off. The representatives of the Southern parties reluctantly accepted these arguments, not so much because they were convinced by them, but because of the lack of anyone else acceptable to the Northern political parties. The Vice-Chancellor of the University of Khartoum was thus appointed.

Fourthly, and more important, there was the problem of who was to represent the South. William Deng, who had already sent a letter to the Prime Minister in November 1964 congratulating the new Government on the overthrow of the military régime,[4] was being challenged by some of his colleagues, who opposed his declared desire to return to the Sudan and his agreement to attend a conference in Juba with a view to solving the Southern problem. Among those who disagreed with William Deng's policy were Aggrey Jaden and Joseph Oduhu. When the Chairman and Secretary-General of the Conference went to Kampala in February to try and persuade the Southern political leaders to participate in the Conference, Joseph Oduhu refused to meet them in either their official or personal capacities. The disagreement and divisions among the Southern political leadership made the convening of the Conference more difficult. It was no use convening a conference if such influential Southern leaders were outside it, and any conclusions reached would lack true force. It was most important that all those who mattered should attend. The Chairman and Secretary-General contacted F. K. Onama, the then Minister of Internal Affairs in Uganda, and explained the position to him. As a result, Onama asked the Southern political leaders in Kampala, including Joseph Oduhu and Aggrey Jaden, to hold a meeting with us, this they did, and he too was present. Aggrey Jaden agreed to attend, and the majority of the other leaders followed.

Similar disagreements arose among the Southern political leadership inside the Sudan. The Southern Front, which had emerged after the October Revolution, proved the most effective among these groups. Other groups which emerged were: (i) the Sudan Unity Party (S.U.P.), led by Santino Deng and Philemon Majok. The former had been Minister of Animal Resources during the six years of General Abboud's régime, and Majok was a member of that régime's Central Council. The S.U.P. advocated a unitary system of government in which local power and authority in the South would be based on tribal divisions. (ii) The Free Southern Front (F.S.F.), led by Buth Diu, a veteran politician who had belonged to the Liberal Party and was an ex-M.P., which held similar views to those of the S.U.P. (iii) The Sudan African Socialist Union (S.A.S.U.) led by Joseph Garang. This party was in fact the Southern branch of the Sudan Communist Party. S.A.S.U., like the Sudan Communist Party, advocated regional autonomy for the South.

None of these groups enjoyed much support in the South. The first two were associated with the unpopular military régime and the third had too few members to be effective. The scene was thus dominated by the Southern Front, which from the beginning was associated with the extreme wing of S.A.N.U. led by Aggrey Jaden and Joseph Oduhu. When differences appeared within S.A.N.U., it set out to oppose William Deng and his policy of co-operation with the Khartoum Government. Like the extreme wing in S.A.N.U. it went out of its way to propose the holding of negotiations outside the Sudan in an African capital when it became clear that they could not be held in Juba.

On the other hand, the Southern Front opposed the representation of any of the other Southern political groups besides itself and S.A.N.U. in the proposed Conference. It warned that it would not attend a Conference which included the representatives of S.U.P. Northern political parties warned that unless points of view other than those of S.A.N.U. and the S.F. were given a chance to be heard in the Conference, they would not attend. Deadlock was averted by a compromise. The Minister of Local Government was asked to appoint nine persons from the South to represent 'the other views'. This later proved unnecessary, as the nine persons once in the Conference declared that they had no views other than those of S.A.N.U. and the S.F.

Looked at in the light of these problems and in the way they had been solved, the very holding of the Conference in itself was an important breakthrough in the North-South relationship.

On 16 March 1965 the Round Table Conference started. For nearly two weeks the delegates discussed the Southern problem. They held sixteen formal meetings and continued the work in sub-committees. At the beginning the atmosphere was tense and it seemed there would never be an agreement; however, it closed on a note of satisfaction. The achievements of the Conference can be summarised as follows.

First, it provided an opportunity and a platform for the political leaders from the North and South to meet together for two weeks and exchange views on the problem of the South. Some of these leaders had never met each other before. There was not only physical but also intellectual contact. Some of the words spoken by the Southerners must have shocked many Northerners, and *vice versa*, but this was exactly what both sides needed. Doubts and suspicions were brought into the open.

Secondly the public addresses and discussions in the Conference contributed to the education of the public outside the conference hall on the problem of the Southern Sudan. Until then few Sudanese in the North and South, whether educated or uneducated, realised the dimensions of the problem or the real grievances of the South. Many facts became known for the first time. Many untrue things were said, but in the final analysis the problem was set in its true historical and political perspective. The reporting of the discussions in the newspapers and on the radio led to a sense of national concern.

Thirdly unlike the Juba Conference of 1947, there was no 'foreign' element directing the discussions or having ready-made solutions. The observers were looked upon not as 'foreigners' but as 'brothers' or 'friends', present in the spirit of African brotherhood. Their attendance produced the feeling among the delegates that the neighbours of the Sudan wanted to see the country unified, not fragmented. Their interventions were welcomed and came as a cooling element to the heated feelings and emotions of the participants. They helped to create and promote a feeling of reconciliation. On the other hand, the discussions provided the observers, all of them responsible persons in the governments or political parties of their own countries, with first-hand information on the problem and on the political leadership of the Sudan.

Fourthly, the resolutions on non-constitutional issues — refugees, famine, security, Southernization, freedom of religion and economic and educational development — were unanimously adopted with no disagreement, which was in itself a great achievement. They pointed to the immediate problems and grievances. They represented a programme of action through which both sides could work to achieve the final solution.

Fifthly the fact that the Conference could not reach a unanimous resolution on the constitutional and administrative issues was taken as a proof of the failure of the Conference. But on close analysis of what had gone on inside the Conference, this judgement is not completely true; it *is* true to say that an agreed and accepted pattern had emerged. The different schemes presented had within them the seeds of an accepted pattern. Delegates realized this towards the end of the Conference. Because of this, they agreed 'to appoint a twelve-man committee to dwell on the constitutional and administrative set-up which will protect the special interest of the South as well as the general interest of the Sudan'.[5]

The phrase 'which will protect the special interest of the South as well as the general interest of the Sudan' in fact combined a phrase used in the Rules of Procedure and the statement issued by the Conference in its fifth meeting. This phrase, on close analysis, meant a rejection at once of separation and of the *status quo*, without this being clearly stated.

However – a sixth point – this was not the whole story. The delegates of the Northern political parties, while agreeing to this part of the resolution, wanted to be sure that the proposed committee would never consider separation. Although the Southern delegates agreed to this, they were not prepared to declare it in public and spell it out in the final resolutions. Their reasons for this were that a public declaration to rule out separation would create further divisions among the Southern political groups; also, Southern political leaders who had not attended the Conference – especially those outside the Sudan – would, in their opinion, use this to discredit those who attended the Conference, and present this as a 'sell-out' to the North; and finally, the Anya Nya, or fighters in the bush, on whom none of those attending the Conference had a strong hold, needed to be contacted first, to avoid any misinterpretation.

Leaders of the Northern political parties could see and appreciate these arguments, but they had their problems too. Northern political opinion was unanimous against separation. Already rumours were being circulated by opposition groups that they were 'selling out' the South to the 'separatist' elements and 'compromising' the unity of the country. Those political groups which were not represented in the transitional Government were using the discussions in the Conference as a lever against the Government. Administrators, army officers, merchants and traders in the South feared that the security situation would deteriorate if the question of separation were not eliminated from any future discussions.

The arguments on both sides were genuine. The fact that they were stated at all among the political leaders indicated the degree of confidence which had grown. A solution had to be found which would allay the fears of both sides, save the Conference and at the same time pave the way for the work of the Twelve-Man Committee.

The solution was found in what came to be known as the 'Special Minute'. It was agreed in a meeting attended by the heads of delegations to draw a secret agreement which would not be made public. The special minute drawn on Monday 29 March 1965, a day before the closing of the Conference, declared:

> 'After discussing the terms of reference of the committee which shall dwell on the constitutional and administrative set-up of the Sudan it was agreed on the statement as drafted but with this clear understanding by all delegates. The terms of the said committee do not include the consideration of the two extremes – that is to say, separation and the *status quo*. The delegates agreed that this be minuted and recorded by all on the direction of the Chairman'.

It was signed by Yousif Mohamed Ali, member of the secretariat.

Thus the Conference had really reached a basic agreement on the future constitutional and administrative relations between the North and the South.

The final important achievement of the Round Table Conference was to appoint the Twelve-Man Committee (six from the North and six from the South) which, in addition to its main purpose of dwelling 'on the issue of the constitutional and administrative set-up which would protect the special interest of the South as well as the general interest of the Sudan'[6] had the following terms of reference: (*a*) to act as a 'watch committee' on the implementation of the steps and policies agreed upon; and (*b*) to plan the normalization of conditions in the South and consider steps for the lifting of the State of Emergency and the establishment of law and order.[7]

The establishment of the Twelve-Man Committee meant that the work of the Conference was not completed, and its objectives had not all been fulfilled. Its tasks were handed to a small committee to carry on the work. The Conference had laid the foundations for the solution of the Southern problem and it was left for the Committee to build on them.

The Committee's twelve members were: Bona Malwal, Natale Olwak and Gordon Abiei, representing the Southern Front; Andrew Wieu, Nikanora Aguer, and Hilary Ochala, representing S.A.N.U.; Mohamed Ahmed Mardi, representing the N.U.P.; Mohamed Dawood Al Khalifa, representing the Umma Party; Al Fatih Abboud, representing the P.D.P.; Dr. Hassan Al Turabi, representing the I.C.F.; Mohamed Ibrahim Nugud, representing the Communist Party; and Sayed Abdalla Al Sayed, representing the Professional Front.

Alternate members were Abel Alier, Lubari Ramba and Hilary Logali for the Southern Front; Joshua Malwal, Andrew W. Ring, Samuel Aru Ball, Ambrose Wol and William Deng for S.A.N.U.; Abdel Latif Al Khalifa for the N.U.P.; Yassin Omer El Imam for the Islamic Charter Front; and Abbas Hamid Nasr for the Umma Party. Yousif Mohamed Ali and Abdel Rahman Abdalla, both members of the Secretariat, were appointed Chairman and Secretary respectively.

The first twelve meetings were occupied with discussions on representation and the question of violence in the South.

Santino Deng of the Sudan Unity Party again tried to get a foothold in the Committee. In a letter to the Prime Minister he asked that his party be represented. His request was naturally turned down by the Committee on the grounds that he had not been represented at the main Conference from which the Committee derived its existence.

The more serious question was that of the representation of S.A.N.U., which Bona Malwal challenged at the first meeting. He produced a telegram from S.A.N.U. in Kampala dismissing William Deng and his group and authorising the S.F. to speak for it. He objected 'to the presence of the three gentlemen occupying S.A.N.U.'s seats in the Committee'.[8] The Southern Front failed to persuade the other members and had to accept the *de facto* situation, since William Deng's S.A.N.U. had been registered in the Sudan as a political party and there was no one to represent S.A.N.U. in Kampala. The Northern parties insisted on not recognising the S.A.N.U. group in Kampala as long as they did not renounce their separatist policy and return to the country. The representatives of William Deng's S.A.N.U. therefore, continued to sit on the Committee until a month later when Peter Akol, one of the S.A.N.U. leaders in Kampala, arrived in Khartoum to inform the Committee that, as far as they were concerned, William Deng did not represent S.A.N.U. This challenge was not accepted by the Northern political parties and the representatives of the home-based S.A.N.U. continued to sit on the Committee.

The second issue which occupied much of the time of the Committee was the question of violence in the South. The representatives of the Communist Party and the People's Democratic Party accused the Southern parties of being responsible for the continuation of hostilities in the South. They suggested that the Twelve-Man Committee should condemn the activities of the Anya Nya and before doing anything else should endeavour to establish peace. When their point of view was rejected by the others, the representatives of both parties absented themselves from the meeting. In July 1965 the P.D.P. representatives withdrew from the Committee, and in August 1965 the Sudan Communist Party also withdrew. From then on the Twelve-Man Committee consisted of the other six political groups.

It would be wrong to explain these withdrawals in terms of the deteriorating conditions of the South. By then, the C.P. and P.D.P. had formed a new alliance – the Socialist Democratic Group – and opposed the Government of Mohamed Ahmed Mahjoub which came to power in June 1967. The P.D.P. had boycotted the elections of the Constitutional Assembly and had no interest in co-operating with the Government to solve the Southern problem through the Twelve-Man Committee.

Notwithstanding the withdrawal of the C.P. and P.D.P., the other members continued to discuss the security situation in the South and the implementation of the resolutions of the Round Table Conference as specified in their terms of reference. All members were unanimous that only through peaceful means would the Southern problem be solved. They were also unanimous in condemning violence. But when it came to condemning the party responsible for violence, they disagreed. While the Northern parties argued that the Anya Nya only should be held responsible, the Southern parties argued that it was the responsibility of both the Anya Nya and the Government security forces. Since no agreement could be reached, the matter was left to rest there.

As for the implementation of the resolutions of the Conference, this was clearly related to the question of

security and the establishment of law and order. The
Southern parties submitted that only through the implementation of the resolution could law and order be established. The Northern point of view was that the resolutions
could not be implemented unless law and order were
established. The official point of view of the Government on
this issue was expressed by the Prime Minister at a meeting
held with the members on 15 January 1966. He said: 'All
that can be implemented under the circumstances now
prevailing in the South has been implemented. Peace centres
have been formed. Southernization of posts was not possible
due to lack of peace. As to the establishment of a university
and new schools, this has also not been possible for the same
reason and we have only been able to re-open old schools in
the last few days'.[9]

Differences of opinion between the Committee members
and the new Government of Mahjoub over the solution of the
Southern problem and the implementation of the resolutions
of the Round Table Conference became serious in June 1966,
when he declared that his Government's proposals for solving
the Southern problem included the establishment of a
regional government in each province to deal with local
affairs, while the central government would be responsible
for foreign affairs, defence, economy, planning and higher
education. He proposed that the regional governments should
consist of a provincial legislature, formed through direct
elections, which would be responsible for elementary and
intermediate education, unspecialized hospitals, roads and
security.[10] This declaration revealed that the attitude of the
new Government was opposed to what had already been
agreed in the Round Table Conference and represented a
departure from the policy of the two major Northern
political parties. Earlier, in March 1966, the Prime Minister
had informed the Constituent Assembly that the Committee
has failed in its task and was 'revolving in a vicious circle'.[11]

The members of the Committee took exception to this:
some considered resigning and others suggested a protest to
the Government. Lubari Ramba expressed the feeling of the
members when he said: 'Since this Government came to
office, its attitude towards the Committee, especially with
regard to encouragement and concern for its word, was not

serious and one feels that it hopes for its failure. Some of the members of the Committee share the same attitude, and this was reflected in their absence from the meetings'.[1][2] It was finally agreed to make a press statement recording the Committee's protest and disagreement with the Prime Minister's statement.[1][3]

This unco-operative attitude on the part of the Government changed when a new Government was formed in July 1966 and Sadig El Mahdi was elected Prime Minister. The latter declared that he fully supported the work of the Twelve-Man Committee, which he described as 'the only serious task that was done during the last eight months, which deserves being proud of'.[1][4]

Meanwhile, and not withstanding all this, the work of the Committee on the constitutional and administrative aspects of its terms of reference continued. At the twelfth meeting held on 18 August, 1965, four schemes were presented by the Southern Front, S.A.N.U., the Islamic Charter Front and the National Unionist Party. The Chairman informed the members that the 'Special Minute' should be read, together with the terms of reference of the Committee and the Round Table Conference resolutions, and that any scheme which advocated separation or preserving the *status quo* should be excluded. Accordingly, the schemes presented by the Southern Front and the I.C.F. were excluded, since the first implied the setting up of a separate state and the second implied preserving the existing constitutional and administrative set-up, namely the centralized system of government.

Later, in September 1965, the Southern Front presented another scheme based on self-determination for the South. This was also rejected.[1][5]

The N.U.P. scheme, which by then had been adopted by the I.C.F. and the Umma Party, proposed the following:

(a) the establishment of regional government in each province with an elected assembly and an executive council;

(b) the regional assemblies to supervise the work of the local authorities;

(c) the regional executive council to have authority over the affairs of the region, e.g. elementary education, public health, forests, etc.

The scheme presented by S.A.N.U. did not differ much

from the one it had presented earlier to the Round Table
Conference. It proposed the following:

(*a*) a federal system based on a Northern region consisting
of the six Northern provinces and a Southern region
consisting of the three Southern provinces;

(*b*) the Southern region to have a legislative council, a
governor, a prime minister and an executive council;

(*c*) the region to have authority on local government
administration, police, prisons, public health, agriculture,
pre-university education, public information, industrial
development, co-operative societies, arms imports and control, export and import, excise duties, roads and regional
communications, courts and the public service.

The two schemes were used as a basis for discussion since
there were points agreed upon in both schemes. Two lists
containing the powers proposed to be within the domain of
the central government and those to be transferred to the
regional government were worked out. By January 1966 the
Committee reached agreement on those powers which would
remain with the centre and those powers which would be
transferred to the region. In the following five months the
discussions included other issues such as the financial
questions, the relationship between the centre and the region,
and the definition and geography of regions. On 26 June
1966, the Twelve-Man Committee submitted its final report
to the Prime Minister.

In its final press statement, the Committee remarked very
appropriately that 'after a year's work, during which the
members fluctuated between feelings of hope and despair',[16]
they were able to find 'a breakthrough' and were convinced
that 'the remaining differences of opinion *were not* fundamental and *could be solved.*[17] According to the statement, they hoped that their proposals would provide 'a
rational basis for reaching the peaceful solution' of the
Southern problem.[18]

But what were 'the remaining differences' which the
Committee referred to and thought were not fundamental?
First, while there was agreement on the establishment of a
legislative assembly, an executive council and an executive
head from among the inhabitants of the region who would be

responsible for both the Centre and the Region, there were differences on the procedure for his appointment. One suggestion was that he should be appointed by the central Government after consultation with the region. The other suggestion was for the regional assembly to offer two candidates from whom the central Government would appoint one. Secondly, while there was agreement on the concept of regional government, there were differences as to its geographical application. The Northern parties suggested the application of the regional rule to all Sudan provinces, i.e. the creation of nine regions in the Sudan. Their main argument for this was: 'If the South is made into one region, this will perpetuate the sense of confrontation between North and South'.[19]

The Southern Parties, which at first suggested the creation of two regions, North and South, agreed later to meet some of the arguments of the Northern delegates and suggested dividing the Sudan into four regions:

South: to be constituted of the three Southern Provinces;
East: to be constituted of Blue Nile and Kassala Provinces;
West: to be constituted of Kordofan and Darfur Provinces;
North: to be constituted of Khartoum and Northern Provinces.

The main argument in support of the South being one region, irrespective of what happened in the North, was that 'any discussion must start by the North and the South as two units because of the differences between them in culture, religion, language and race'.[20] They also argued that 'the South considers itself as a unit and the Southern citizens have expressed their wish to remain as a unit. The basic duty is to solve the Southern problem, and this necessitates giving this fact due consideration and not making the South as other parts of the country where no such problem has arisen, or not to the extent of the Southern problem'.[21]

It was this last point which the Northern parties feared. Already some regional groupings had appeared after the 1965 elections. These included the Beja Congress, the Nuba Mountains Association and a group consisting of some Darfur M.P.s. It is true that the problems they posed did not have

the same dimension as the Southern problem. The establishment of a Southern Region would, in the opinion of the
Northern parties, have promoted the concept of regionalism
and might have led to further fragmentations of the country.
Since no unanimous agreement was reached on this point it
was decided to state both proposals and not make specific
positive recommendations.

Three other issues on which the Southern Front insisted,
but which were rejected by the Northern parties, concerned
educational policy, cultural relations with other countries and
the formation of a home guard. On educational policy, the
Southern Front suggested that the region should be given the
opportunity to plan its own policy of education; on cultural
relations, it should have the right to establish cultural
relations with other countries independently from the central
Government; and on the home guard, it should have the right
to establish a militia to assist the security forces. The
Committee noted the first proposal but rejected the other
two.[2 2]

One issue which had taken up much of the Committee's
time but which was not reflected in the final report was the
issue of financial and economic relations. Senior Government
officers dealing with finance and planning were interviewed
by the Committee and each side submitted a memorandum
on the issues of taxation and planning. The points of
agreement and disagreement were:[2 3]

(a) The Southern parties suggested that taxation should be
the concern of the regions. The Northern parties disagreed
since this would imply the establishment of a federal system
which they had already rejected. They opposed the granting
of financial independence to the regions.

(b) The Southern parties restricted the authority of the
central Government only to import and export duties. The
regions should, in their view, be responsible for the fixing of
rates and taxes and collecting and spending the revenue from
all other taxes, and would contribute to the budget of the
central Government. The Northern parties suggested that all
taxes must be placed under the authority of the centre. In
their view this was a necessity in an under-developed country
where the limited resources were to be distributed equally

among the regions and where the central Government undertook all major projects. They did not, however, object to the delegation by the centre to the regions of the power to fix any of the taxes, their collection or spending.

(*c*) Both agreed that taxation provisions should not be embodied in the constitution, but should be dealt with in a series of agreements so as to secure flexibility.

(*d*) Both agreed that the central Government was the ultimate authority on taxation.

As they were not able to reach a decision, the Committee recommended the establishment of a committee of experts to make recommendations. They agreed that a central development committee should be set up together with regional sub-committees for the purposes of planning and development.

It can be seen that the achievements of the Twelve-Man Committee were far from insignificant. Despite the political changes which had taken place, sometimes amounting to political crises and despite the withdrawal of the representatives of the P.D.P. and Communist Party which diluted the National representation of the Committee, the lack of public interest in its work and the unsympathetic attitude of the Prime Minister at the time, the Committee was able to fulfil at least one of its terms of reference, namely 'to dwell on the issue of the constitutional and administrative set-up which will protect the special interest of the South as well as the general interest of the Sudan'.[24]

It is true that the members did not agree on all points, but the differences were not fundamental. It was not able to carry out the other two functions: to act as a watch committee on the implementation of the steps and policies agreed upon and to plan the normalization of conditions in the South. It had, at least, tried. Its failure to carry out this task was due more to the unco-operative attitude of the Government and of the Southern politicians outside the country than to the members of the Committee. The re-convening of the Round Table Conference as specified in its resolution was a function of the Government and not of the Committee.

The Committee held forty-eight meetings, sitting for more

than a year; it interviewed senior government officers and considered a variety of schemes and proposals.

Like the Round Table Conference, the meetings of the Committee provided each side with an opportunity to have greater insight into the thinking of the other and better understanding of the issues. Its work was in this sense another positive step forward in the search for a solution of the Southern problem. Had the Committee failed it would have meant that the Round Table Conference had been a failure since its task was to complete what had been started a year previously. The uncompleted parts of its task were more complex and difficult than the working-out on paper – very important in itself – of a constitutional and administrative set-up. The achievement of peace and development was a function of the whole political development of the country rather than the work of committee members sitting in Khartoum.

REFERENCES

1 M. O. Beshir, *The Southern Sudan; Background to Conflict*, Hurst, London, 1968, and Khartoum University Press, 1970.

2. For example, see Oliver Albino, *The Sudan: a Southern Viewpoint*, Oxford University Press, 1970; M. A. Salih, 'The Round Table Conference and The Search for a Solution to the Problem of the Southern Sudan 1964–1969', M.Sc. thesis, University of Khartoum, 1971; and Dunstan M. Wai (ed.), *The Southern Sudan: the Problem of National Integration*, Frank Cass, London 1973.

3. Albino, *op. cit.*, p. 56.

4. Beshir, *op. cit.*, Appendix 10, p. 154.

5. Beshir, *op. cit.*, Appendix 19, pp. 183–5.

6. *Ibid.*

7. *Ibid.*

8. Minutes of first meeting of Twelve-Man Committee, 22 May 1965.

9. Minutes of the 33rd meeting of Twelve-Man Committee, 15 January 1966.

10. *Al Rai Al'am* newspaper, Khartoum, 10 June 1960, quoted M. A. Salih, *op. cit.*, pp. 200–1.

11. Minutes of the 40th meeting of Twelve-Man Committee, 6 March 1966.

12. *Ibid.*

13. Press statements, 8 March 1966 attached to minutes of 41st meeting of Twelve-Man Committee, 9 March 1968.

14. Quoted Salih, *op. cit.*, p. 201.

15. Minutes of 19th meeting of Twelve-Man Committee, 30 September 1965.

16. Minutes of 48th meeting of Twelve-Man Committee, 12 June 1966.

17. *Ibid.*

18. *Ibid.*

19. Report of Twelve-Man Committee, Khartoum.

20. *Ibid.*

21. *Ibid.*

22. *Ibid.*

23. Minutes of 38th meeting of Twelve-Man Committee, 19 February 1966.

24. Resolutions of the Round Table Conference, Appendix 19, in Beshir, *op. cit.*, pp. 183—5.

CHAPTER II

POLITICAL DEVELOPMENTS AND THE SOUTHERN QUESTION 1965-1969

As the Twelve-Man Committee was preparing for its work, the Government of Sir Al Khatim Al Khalifa, under pressure from the Umma and National Unionist parties – the two major political groups – decided to hold elections for a new parliament.

The last parliamentary elections had been held in 1958. The military régime had continued from 1958 to 1964 when it was overthrown by a popular revolt, in which the problems of the Southern Sudan and opposition to the measures applied to them by the military regime, figured prominently. Leaders of the political parties, especially the Muslim Brothers and the Communists, had been critical of the repressive measures applied. The North, for the third time since the Juba Conference in 1947 and the mutiny of the Southern Corps in 1955, demonstrated its concern with what was happening in the Southern Sudan.[1]

The appointment of Sir Al Khatim Al Khalifa as Prime Minister was particularly popular with many Southerners. He had worked long in the South and was personally known to them. The appointment of Clement Mboro, who later became President of the Southern Front, and Ezboni Mondiri was hailed by both Northerners and Southerners as a positive step towards the solution of the Southern problem. The first had advocated unity in the Juba Conference and the second was supported by the younger generation among the extremists. The Prime Minister's declaration that the Southern problem was 'the most urgent national issue of our time', which therefore had to be 'tackled very quickly and energetically',[2] and his admission that 'force is no solution to this vital problem which has so many facets, social, economic and cultural',[3] paved the way for the Round Table Conference and later the Twelve-Man Committee.[4] On the other hand the decision to hold the elections for a new parliament posed many problems – the most important of which was whether it was opportune and possible to hold them in the South. The issue was further complicated by the fact that the Round Table Conference had not made specific recommendations on the constitutional and administrative set-up for the South, and the Twelve-Man Committee had not started its work. The security situation in the South made it impossible to hold elections outside the town.

The two major political parties, however, were determined to hold elections irrespective of the situation in the South, and of the political implication in terms of future political relations between North and South. They advocated the holding of elections in the North and their postponement in the South until conditions were better, but this was rejected by both S.A.N.U. and the Southern Front. The People's Democratic Party and the Communist Party were also opposed to the elections, arguing that elections in only one part of the country would promote the case of the separatists and lead to a deterioration in the security situation. The Supreme Council, to which the matter was referred, ruled that no elections should be held in the South until the emergency laws were removed. It agreed, however, that elections could be held in the North. Luigi Adwok, who represented the South on the Supreme Council, and who had been assured of his continuation on the Supreme Council and the representation of the Southern Front in any new government, gave his casting vote in a divided Council in favour of holding elections in the North to be followed later by elections in the South. Faced with this situation, S.A.N.U. and the Southern Front issued a joint statement demanding guarantees from the Government on the following points: that the political parties in the North and the South would continue their efforts to implement Round Table Conference resolutions, the forthcoming parliament would not make legislation for the South, and the three cabinet seats held by the Southerners (Interior, Communications and Works) would continue to be so.[5] The Southern Front in a separate statement demanded that the three Southern ministers would be nominated by the South – meaning of course the Southern Front and S.A.N.U.

But both issues – elections and representation – were soon challenged. Twenty-one candidates had already been nominated in the Southern constituencies, and when Parliament met they demanded to be seated in Parliament on the grounds that the decisions of the Supreme Council on this issue were illegal. Their claim was upheld by the Supreme Court, and the twenty-one candidates – most of them Northerners claiming to represent the South – were seated in Parliament. They were drafted into the ranks of Umma and the National Unionist parties. At the insistence of Mohamed Ahmed Mahjoub, the Prime Minister, on representing other Southern political parties in his cabinet, contrary to previous agreement, the Southern Front withdrew its candidates for the Supreme Council and the Cabinet. In their place, Philemon Majok, who had participated in the Juba Conference of 1947 and later joined Santino Deng in the Sudan Unity Party, becoming a delegate to the Round Table Conference as a Government nominee, was appointed to the Supreme Council to represent the South. Andrew Wieu and Alfred Wol, who both belonged to William Deng's S.A.N.U. became ministers but resigned upon the appointment of Buth Diu, a veteran Southern politician and founder member of the old Liberal Party, on the grounds that the earlier agreements with the Mahjoub Government were not honoured. The Southern problem was once again caught up in the political game of the Northern Sudan.

In his first address to Parliament Mahjoub declared that his Government would continue to seek a peaceful democratic solution to the Southern problem, and would end 'the policy of appeasement and leniency in dealing with the outlaws and those who support them. It will order complete disbandment of arms, and end completely the fanatic bands that play with security. It will order the army to follow the criminals, return the state of law and order and punish the mutineers'.[6] This was clearly a reversal of the policy followed by the previous government which had followed a policy of appeasement, reconciliation and negotiation, and for that purpose had released the political prisoners and instructed the army not to act except in self-defence. The new policy was justified on the grounds that the previous policy had resulted in increased activity by the Anya Nya and the deterioration of the security situation. This was not far from the truth.

The Anya Nya, on whom there was little control from the politicians, exploited the situation to advance its cause. Members of the Southern Front and S.A.N.U. in the South exploited the liberal policy advanced by the transitional government to show their hostility to the North. Neither the army nor the administration in the South was happy with the situation, and both therefore welcomed the change of policy.

The result of all this was an increase in activity on the part of the army and more bloodshed, especially among the civilian population. These activities reached their climax in the Juba and Wau incidents of 8 and 11 July respectively. A report by a judge of the High Court of Appeal in Khartoum later found 'abundant evidence and beyond any reasonable doubt'[7] that the incidents had taken place, and estimated the number killed at 430. The report criticized the Government for engaging in a 'high-handed, illegal and most inhuman act'.[8]

It would be wrong to assume that the civil authorities had condoned the way the army had acted in these and other cases. A report of the Ministry of Interior in February 1966 criticized the Army authorities in the South and advocated self-control and the punishment of those who committed irresponsible acts.

Besides stepping up military activity against the Anya Nya, the Government set out to implement certain administrative measures: a committee for the resettlement of returning refugees was established, and 'peace villages' were organised to receive the refugees or those who had fled from the countryside. Special camps were established for Congolese refugees to prevent the Anya Nya contacting them. The transportation of arms through the Sudan to the Congo rebels, which had taken place in the past, was stopped.

Appeals for peace were broadcast from Radio Omdurman. In addition, the Ministry of Works started to rebuild and maintain roads and bridges. Facilities for medical care were increased and more doctors were sent from the North to the South. In order to encourage Northerners to work in the South, special financial allowances were offered.

These efforts on the military and civil side were accompanied by diplomatic efforts. One of Mahjoub's first actions was to affirm the Sudan's future adherence to the O.A.U. pledges on non-interference in other nations' affairs. An agreement was reached with Ethiopia in July 1965, and this was followed by a goodwill visit to East Africa. The aim of the visits was to explain the Government's efforts in solving the Southern problem, to persuade neighbouring countries not to assist the rebels and to reach agreements on the return of refugees. The governments of Kenya, Tanzania and Uganda gave assurances that they would not allow the refugees and politicians to engage in subversive activities. However, relations with Chad and Ethiopia were not as friendly as the Mahjoub government would have wished. In August 1966 President Tombalbaye of Chad accused the Sudan of assisting the Chadian rebels and allowing them to operate from Darfur. The allegations were denied by the Sudan Government; admitting only that it had given medical treatment to the wounded. The Chadian Government closed the border and put all the Sudanese residents in Chad under restriction, and relations between the two countries became tense. President Diori of Niger intervened and mediated between them, and by the end of the year relations were back to normal.

Ethiopian-Sudanese relations also passed through difficult times. First there was the border dispute. Ethiopia continued to claim that she was not party to the agreement on the international borders signed by the British and their representative at the beginning of the century; Ethiopia pressed for a revision of the borders and a new agreement. Secondly, there was the dispute over Fashala which arose out of the first problem. In April 1965 there were reports of Ethiopian farmers moving 45 miles inside the Sudan with their tractors. There were protests from the Sudan and the problem remained unsolved.

Then there was the problem of the Eritrean refugees and the activities of the Eritrean Liberation Front. The Ethiopians accused the Sudan of harbouring the rebels and even of giving them assistance. Their accusations were strengthened by the continuous hostility of both the Communists and Muslim Brotherhood press and by the discovery of arms being smuggled from Syria to the Eritrean rebels. Two ministers, one from the Islamic Charter Front and one from the National Unionist Party, were accused of being involved in the smuggling of arms.

The relations between the Sudan and Ethiopia continued to be tense until the Border Commission was revived and both sides agreed not to encourage subversive activities against each other. But despite the agreements reached and the improvement in relations with neighbouring countries, reports received in the Sudan revealed that the Anya Nya were still receiving arms and other assistance from outside through neighbouring countries. Reports also indicated that although neighbouring governments – in Ethiopia, Uganda, Kenya and Central Africa – were not officially involved, some of their high-ranking officials were. This was confirmed by William Deng when he stated in April 1966 that despite the agreements and understandings which had been reached, Southern politicians continued to receive support from 'high officials in the neighbouring countries'.[9] They continued to move freely in these countries, discouraging the refugees from returning and arranging for arms to be smuggled in the South. The first year after the Round Table Conference, therefore, did not witness any significant improvement in the situation in spite of internal and external efforts. The only bright aspect was the work of the Twelve-Man Committee.

When Sadig El Mahdi replaced Mahjoub as Prime Minister, one of his first actions was to remove Buth Diu from the Cabinet and appoint Arop Yor Ayik and Jervase Yak as ministers. Both were civil servants, and their appointment was looked upon as an appeasement of S.A.N.U. and the moderates. His second important act in relation to the South was his calling of a Political Parties' Conference in October 1966 to reach an agreement on the report of the Twelve-Man Committee whose work he had already praised. All the political parties in the country – fifteen of them – with the exception of the Communist Party, which was banned at the time, were invited. The Sudan Unity Party and the Free Southern Front were among the political parties participating in the Conference. Neither S.A.N.U. nor the Southern Front objected to their participation, since this was not a Round Table Conference or a Twelve-Man Committee to determine the relations between the North and South, but a conference to discuss less important issues arising from these reports. After all, Northern political parties with weight were participating.

The P.D.P., the Islamic Socialist Party and the Republican Party refused to participate on the grounds that they rejected in principle the report of the Twelve-Man Committee. The Islamic Charter Front later withdrew as well.

Mohamed Salih Al Shingeiti, a veteran Umma Party politician who took part in the Juba Conference of 1947 and became Speaker of Parliament in 1958, was elected Chairman of the Conference. The terms of reference for the Conference were laid down by the Prime Minister as follows: 1. to consider the points of difference in the Twelve-Man Committee report: the regional geography and the procedure for electing the regional governor; and 2. to recommend whether the Round Table Conference should be re-convened to consider the report of the Twelve-Man Committee, or whether the matter should be referred to the Constitution Committee.

On the question of the geography of the regions, the Northern parties continued with the stand they had made in the Twelve-Man Committee, i.e. the creation of nine regions based on the existing provincial administrative divisions. S.A.N.U. and the Southern Front likewise continued their previous stand, i.e. the three Southern provinces to be amalgamated into one region. The Sudan Unity Party supported the creation of nine regions. The Beja Congress and the Nuba Mountains Association supported the same, provided that Kordofan, Kassala and Darfur provinces would be subdivided to create three more regions in the country. After a lengthy discussion a compromise was arrived at. The Sudan would be divided into nine regions: these divisions would be reconsidered after the lapse of five years – which however, would not prevent any two or more regions amalgamating together if they so desired.

On the issue of the appointment of regional governors the following was agreed: the central Government would nominate three persons of whom the regional assembly would choose one. In case none of them were acceptable to the region, a second list of three nominees would be made by the central government and the region would elect one of them. It was further agreed that the proposed system would be reconsidered after five years. The Southern Front reserved its position and insisted that the governor of the region (the region's head executive) should be elected by the region and appointed by the Head of State.

As for reconvening the Round Table Conference, the general feeling was that the time was inopportune. The Government of Sadig El Mahdi was keen on the making of a new constitution for the Sudan and having it approved as soon as possible. With this in mind, it was decided to hold elections in the South – including the thirty-six Southern constituencies where elections had not been held in 1965 – in March 1967. The Southern Front boycotted the elections on the grounds that it was impossible to hold them while the state of emergency existed; it argued that elections should be held after an agreement had been reached on a new constitution. S.A.N.U. the Unity Party and the Liberal Party participated in the elections, with the following results: Umma Party 15, S.A.N.U. 10, National Unionist Party 5, Independents 3, Unity Party 2, Liberal Party 1. Among the Southern leaders returned to Parliament were William Deng (S.A.N.U.), Luigi Adwok (Independent) and Buth Diu (Liberal Party).

The period of elections in the South coincided with the completion of the work of the Political Parties Conference and the establishment of the National Constitution Commission, whose work began on 12 February 1967. The National Constitution Commission consisted of representatives of the Northern Political Parties and representatives of S.A.N.U., the Southern Front, the Sudan Unity Party, the Liberal Party and the Southern National Peace Party. The last two were offshoots of the Free Southern Front, previously led by Buth Diu. In addition to these, seven Northerners and four Southerners (Luigi Adwok, Arop Yor Ayik, Joshua Malwal and Abdel Nabi Abdel Gadir Mursal) were appointed to the Commission.

The National Constitution Commission completed its work in January 1968 and submitted its recommendations to the Constituent Assembly. Mohamed Ahmed Mahjoub had by then returned to become Prime Minister after the government of Sadig Al Mahdi was defeated in May 1967. His Cabinet included representatives of the Southern Front and a new faction of S.A.N.U. led by Alfred Wol. William Deng and Sadig Al Mahdi had retreated to the opposition benches.

Rules of procedure, once again, occupied much of the time of the National Constitution Commission. The Northern parties proposed that decisions should be made on the basis of one vote per delegate and by a simple majority. S.A.N.U. and the Southern Front, being the minority, suggested that decisions should be by consensus rather than by majority voting. Their suggestion was not accepted.

When the question of regional government was discussed, the Committee agreed to consider three documents: the report and recommendations of the Twelve-Man Committee, the report and recommendations of the Political Parties Conference, and a note on regionalism prepared by the Technical Committee of the National Constitution Conference.

The proposal by S.A.N.U., the Southern Front, the Beja Congress and the Nuba Mountains Association to adopt the reports and recommendations contained in the two first documents on regional government and embody them in the constitution was rejected. Instead it was agreed to propose the creation of nine regions in the country. The method of appointment of the regional governor again became an issue of disagreement. The proposal of the Southerners to provide in the constitution for the election of two vice-presidents, one of whom would be from the South, was not accepted. Instead the draft constitution provided for the appointment by the President of a governor-general for each region out of a list of three persons to be nominated by him and supported by the Regional Council, i.e. the same proposal already rejected by S.A.N.U. and the Southern Front in the Twelve-Man Committee.

Two issues which received a great deal of attention and often led to heated discussions were the financial relations between the centre and the regions, and the position of the civil service in the regional government. When agreement was not possible on these two points, it was decided to regulate them in separate laws.

The other issue which caused a great deal of disagreement and nearly led to the breaking up of the National Constitution Commission related to the place of Islam and Sharia law in the Sudan Constitution. The proposal of the Islamic Charter Front, supported by the Umma Party and the N.U.P., that the constitution should clearly and specifically state that 'the Sudan is an Islamic Republic' was rejected by the delegates from the South and Nuba Mountains Association. As a compromise, and with the reservations of the Southern Front, S.A.N.U. and other Southern delegates, it was agreed on the following formula: 'The Sudan is a Democratic Socialist Republic based on Islam.'[10]

Another controversial issue related to the decision to state in the constitution that the Sudan is 'an integral part of the Arab Islamic and African Entity'.[11] The Southern Front's proposed amendment that the Sudan is 'an integral part of the Afro-Arab entity'[12] was rejected by the National Constitution Commission. The Southern members failing to get their amendments and proposals accepted continued their opposition to the proposed draft constitution inside Parliament. They presented amendments which would delete or cancel articles referring to Islam, Sharia and the Arabic language together with articles defining the Sudan as a unitary state. As the Government was keen to get the constitution approved, and the support of the Southern M.P.s and their allies (about forty) was vitally necessary, a compromise was reached. The latter did not meet all the objectives but it diluted the phrases on Islam, Sharia and the Arabic language, while at the same time giving recognition to Christianity and the use of the English language.[13]

The political crises that followed did not, however, allow for the approval of the draft constitution. Parliament was dissolved in February 1968, and elections for a new Parliament were held in April 1968. In these elections S.A.N.U. won 15 seats, the Southern Front 10 seats and the Nile Unity Party, led by Philemon Majok, 1 seat. Mahjoub was returned as Prime Minister with a new coalition government made up from the Democratic Unionist Party, the Umma (Al Hadi Al Mahdi's faction) and the Southern Front. The latter was represented in the Cabinet by Clement Mboro and Hilary Paul Logali. A new National Constitution Committee was formed to revise the draft constitution already proposed and submit it to a new constituent assembly or Parliament. The new National Constitution Commission did not, however, achieve much, and there were more political crises. New political groupings and alliances were formed, which finally led to worse political chaos.

These crises which had characterized the political life of the Sudan since 1966 did not contribute to the normalization of conditions in the South or the improvement of the security situation. It was true that the discussions and recommendations of the Political Parties Conference and the National Constitution Commission had clarified the issues involved and achieved compromises, but the changes of government and party alliances had reduced the effectiveness of these achievements. The divisions in the Umma Party and in S.A.N.U., the changing position of the Southern Front from opposition to Mahjoub's Government to support for it, the further fragmentation of Southern opinion through the appearance of new political groups, and the appearance of new regional groups such as the Beja Congress and the Nuba Mountains Association all contributed to the prevailing political chaos.

The insistence of the major political parties — the Umma and Democratic Unionist Party with the Islamic Charter Front — on an Islamic constitution introduced new and complicated issues into the Southern question. These and other factors which we discuss in the following chapters did not promote conditions of peace in the South. *Vigilant*, the newspaper published by the Southern Front in Khartoum, wrote in January 1967 that 'the situation in the Southern Sudan continues to be what it was two years ago despite the public utterances in Khartoum that the situation has returned to normal'.[14] This was confirmed by a delegation of the People's Democratic Party which visited the South in the same month and later reported its findings to the Government. The report cited the various incidents as proof of the prevailing insecurity.[15] The following consists of extracts from the report.

Equatoria
On 20 October 1966 the rebels demolished bridges between Nimule and Juba. On 24 October they destroyed bridges between Tali and Tekaka, and on 28 October they attacked Ghoremia Village, 4 miles from Kapoeta, killing three men and three women, and burning some huts. On 2 November the rebels destroyed a military tank six miles outside Juba as an army convoy was passing. On 7 November the rebels destroyed a tank, killed four soldiers, wounded nine and captured a mortar. At Iba, in the Meridi area, the army was attacked by rebels and a corporal was killed. On 19 December the rebels attacked the village of Daloka in Kapoeta district, killed four soldiers, stole four head of cattle and abducted a number of women. On 29 December the army clashed with the citizens of Lernyo village.

Bahr el Ghazal
In December the rebels attacked the hospital at Rumbek with stones, broke in and carried away medical supplies. On the Rumbek-Meridi road, the rebels attacked a Jur village and killed about ninety persons. They destroyed a convoy from Rumbek at Chueibet police post. On 18 January 1967 Rumbek town was exposed to constant attacks by the rebels, in one of which the rebels killed seven workers in the Ministry of Works labour camps, a few miles from Rumbek. On 21 January the rebels attacked a police car at Mboro police post and killed seven policemen and four civilians, wounding two policemen and one child. The wounded are in Wau Hospital now. The rebels captured eight guns and four motor-guns and 1,200 rounds of ammunition in this one incident. They also carried away the police uniforms and burned the car. On 14 January the rebels attacked a convoy in Chueibet wounding five soldiers. The convoy was attacked at a teak plantation 5 miles from Wau Town on its way from Tonj.

On 1 January between Mbior and Maber railway stations in Aweil district, the rebels attacked villages, despite the heavy police force there. At the end of January about fifty rebels attacked Aweil town and captured more than 200 head of cattle. The rebels also set on fire a number of houses in Aweil town, which was under curfew from 6 p.m. till morning. At the end of January the rebels attacked Chueibet police post. There was a whole company of the army and some police and they wounded a soldier.

On 22 January the army attacked an Anya Nya group, 2 miles out of Wau town, killed six Anya Nya, and captured ten with a quantity of arms. On 1 February the rebels arrested two men, one called Bol Madut and a friend of his. They cut off the ears of the two men and they were in hospital. On 3 January the rebels attacked the house of Honga Jamus in Wau town and wounded him. He was in hospital. In December the rebels kidnapped a chief and a court president of Wau town. The rebels made several attempts to capture arms from the police in Wau town.

Upper Nile Province
Six chiefs are still under detention. They were accused by the authorities of co-operation with the rebels. The rebels were in full control of the district and had thrown a ring round the town. The police posts outside the town were closed down. A number of clashes took place between the rebels and the army during the visit of the Prime Minister, who could not travel anywhere in the South except by plane or under heavy army escort.

A Northern Sudanese living in the South at the time summarized the situation as follows:[16]

The situation has improved but not to the extent that can permit any talk of elections that would be free and democratic.
(a) The number of bridges that have been destroyed by the rebels west of the Nile in Equatoria province – i.e. in Juba-Yei, Juba-Meridi, Yambio, Anzara, Tombura – is about thirty. None of them has been repaired up till now. Transport to the area has been limited. Even if we wanted to believe that the rebels no longer existed, these bridges alone create more than just a problem.

(*b*) East of the Nile in Equatoria, the rebels have blown up four main bridges on the Juba-Torit and Juba-Nimule roads.
(*c*) From a whole area like the Shakeri hills the Government has been forced out completely. The rebels are not only living there, but they have *dura* cultivations and clean water supply guarded by a rebel force.
(*d*) The week before last alone witnessed a number of clashes with the rebels in the districts of the towns at Khor Englizi and at Yirol in Bahr el Ghazal province.

In the Yirol area the rebels burnt the steamer of the Survey Department. In the Bor area of Upper Nile province, there also occurred an incident. The outskirts of Wau was the scene of an exchange of fire between the security forces and the rebels on 3 January 1967. The rebels also opened fire on a motor trolley of the Wau railway line between Pango and Kangi stations. The Government forces attacked a rebel camp about 20 miles east of Meridi town. In Upper Nile Province the security forces destroyed a rebel court in Kur area while it was in session.

Thus life in the Southern Sudan returned to the pattern it had known before 1964. The army pursued the rebels, while the latter attacked police posts and army convoys. Villagers in the countryside and innocent people were killed. This led to an increasing number of people in the countryside being forced to leave their homes and take refuge in neighbouring countries or in the towns, or in any places where there was police protection.

It became evident during this period that the rebels were directing their activities not only against the army and police but also against the villagers in outlying districts and against what they called 'co-operators'. Their attacks against the villagers were for the purpose of obtaining food and clothing. As food became scarce, cases were reported of the rebels rounding up cattle. These attacks led in some areas to reluctance on the part of the villagers and chiefs to provide information or co-operation to the authorities. In other cases it led to the formation of 'home guards' by the villagers to protect their villages. The reluctant ones feared reprisals from the rebels, but the 'home guard' acted against the rebels.

During April-June 1967 the 'home guards' in Aweil, Rumbek and Tonj arrested one rebel, killed two others and handed over their arms to the Government authorities. In some cases the actions of the 'home guards' did not receive the support of the whole tribe, or of other neighbouring tribes which had not suffered from similar attacks, or which were strong though secret supporters of the rebels.

Another new feature of the rebel activities during this period was their attacks on returning refugees. In June 1967 they attacked a bus transporting refugees returning from Uganda to the Sudan, killed the Ugandan driver and wounded two refugees. Their aim was to frighten and discourage those who had decided for one reason or another to return to the Sudan.

These activities by the rebels and counteractivities by the army and police continued during the following year. Conditions differed from one province to another. In Equatoria, for example, there was a relative improvement in the situation in Juba, Kapoeta, Yambio and Tombura. Torit and Meridi districts were less peaceful. In Bahr el Ghazal there were no less than 343 incidents in 1968. The worst affected area was that of Aweil. In Upper Nile province the worst affected districts were Kadok, Nasir, Bor and Fashala. Conditions in the Renk area had improved to the extent that the army unit there was withdrawn.

The most tragic event during this period was the murder of William Deng, President of S.A.N.U., together with six of his supporters in an ambush on the Rumbek-Wau road on 5 May 1968. The Government accused the rebels of the murder, but the latter denied this and put the blame on the army. An investigation was ordered by the Government, but no report is yet available. The murder of William Deng represented a great setback in North-South relations. Only those opposed to a peaceful solution or to his leadership would have benefited from it. Deng's decision to return to the Sudan in 1965 to attend the Round Table Conference and his participation in that event, in the Twelve-Man Committee, in the Political Parties Conference and in the National Constitution Commission had all made a positive contribution to the search for a solution of the Southern problem.

Another event which had resulted from the offensive action by the army and counter-offensives by the rebels was the murder of Father Saturnino Lohure on 23 January 1967. Fr. Saturnino was a member of the Sudan Parliament in 1958 and had taken refuge in Uganda and become active in Southern Sudanese politics outside the Sudan; had come to be looked upon as the father-figure of the Southern Sudanese political and refugee organisations, and was in charge of most of the foreign aid received by the rebels. The Government claimed that Father Saturnino was killed by the army in one of its operations against the rebels, but this was denied by the Southern Front, and his murder was attributed to the Ugandan forces in one of their operations near the Sudan-Uganda border. The Southern Front went out of its way and sent a letter to President Obote informing him that Fr. Saturnino was seen on 23 January 1967 'in the hands of the Ugandan Army in Kitgum. Two days later his body was found gutted with bullets on the side of the road at the Uganda town of Luking'.[17]

The Southern Front asked President Obote, 'in keeping with the spirit of the international law governing the treatment of refugees',[18] to form an investigating committee to look into the case. They informed him that in the absence of a satisfactory explanation, they would conclude that the Ugandan armed forces would be made responsible for the death of 'a man beloved and respected by his people in the Southern Sudan'.[19]

Notwithstanding all this, army and police reports at the time made it plain that there was a slight improvement in the security situation towards the end of 1968 compared to the previous two years. This could be accounted for by several factors. First, the policy, already started in 1966, of allowing the army to take the offensive, attack the rebels and pursue them placed the rebels on the defensive. The army, which was better equipped through arms bought from West Germany, was under instructions to be careful when making its operations not to alienate the civilian population. It was directed to co-operate with the police, the administrators and, whenever possible, the chiefs and 'home guards'. In addition, the army was directed, when not involved in

operations, to provide guards for the protection of aero-
dromes, steamers, railways, bridges, convoys, state buildings
and possessions, post offices and communication installa-
tions. This policy enabled the army to carry out a series of
successful operations against the rebels and, relatively speak-
ing, to win the confidence of those who were fed up
with the war or reluctant to become involved in it.

Secondly, the Government set out to promote friendly
relations with the governments of Uganda, Ethiopia, Congo
and the Central African Republic – the countries in which
many Sudanese refugees resided and where Southern political
leaders were engaged in hostile activities against the Sudan.
The degree of success differed from one country to the other.

Uganda at first agreed to co-operate to the extent of
conducting joint operations, by the Sudanese army and the
Ugandan armed forces, against the rebels. The refugees were
removed away from the borders and the Southern political
leaders were warned against carrying on hostile activities
against the Sudan. In some cases those who continued them
were arrested. However, this policy and attitude of the
Ugandan Government did not continue for long. By 1968 the
Sudanese authorities were complaining, with justice, of the
non-cooperation of the Uganda Government. This was
attributed to pressure from Church groups, and to certain
Ugandan ministers and officers known for their sympathies
with the rebels.

Ethiopia, with whom the Sudan had border problems,
continued unofficially to support the rebels. The refugees
and the Southern politicians continued their hostile activities
in spite of repeated protests by the Sudan Government. On
the diplomatic level, the Ethiopian Foreign Minister was
invited to the Sudan in December 1966, and the Sudan
Foreign Minister visited Ethiopia in January 1967. The aim
of these visits was to persuade the Ethiopians not to allow
the Southern political leaders living in Ethiopia to engage in
activities directed against the Sudan. Ethiopia had always
accused the Sudan of harbouring Eritrean rebels, and
co-operation was not forthcoming. The Emperor's visit to the
Sudan in February 1967 was not well received by the Muslim
Brothers, the Communists, the People's Democratic Party
and the Arab Socialists who demonstrated against him.

Ethiopian suspicions increased, and thus there was no common ground for co-operation. Upper Nile province continued to suffer from the incursion of the Sudanese rebels from the Ethiopian border and from around Gambaila.

In addition to the support and assistance given by Ethiopia to the rebels, there were reports of activity by the Israeli Embassy in Addis Ababa on behalf of the rebels, to which the Ethiopians were turning a blind eye. The Ethiopian Government also ignored the activities of those missionaries and church organisations in their country active in the promotion of the rebels' cause. At one time, the Ethiopians were accused of permitting aeroplanes to fly from Ethiopia or through it with arms for the rebels.

The Congo Kinshasa Government and Sudanese representatives had an opportunity for discussion during the Conference of Heads of State of the East and Central African countries, and it was agreed to assist the refugees who wished to return to the Southern Sudan. However, Congo had its own problems with the Sudan: a number of Congolese refugees had already settled in the Southern Sudan, and although they were not involved in activities directed against it, yet the Congo Government continued to press the Sudan Government for their repatriation. Catholic Church organisations in the Congo continued to give aid and support to the Southern Sudan rebels.

The situation in the Central African Republic was no different from that in the Congo. There were about 20,000 Sudanese refugees there, and the rebels had established training camps on the country's border with the Sudan. No efforts were made to discourage these activities, and the authorities in the Sudan continued to complain of the passive attitude of the Central African Republic Government.

The Sudan's neighbours to the North presented a different situation. In Egypt there were no Southern Sudanese refugees. Cairo had always been a 'home' for Third World revolutionaries and for statesmen and politicians expelled from their countries for one reason or another, but it was not seen by the Southern political leaders as an appropriate place from which to carry on hostile activities: Egypt and the Arab world were equated with the Northern Sudan.

The Sudan's membership of the Arab League was always

frowned upon by Southern leaders. As the Sudan's support for the Palestinian cause and for Egypt grew, Israel turned more against the Sudan and in support of the rebels. On the other hand, the rebels' contact with Israel increased, as did their opposition to the involvement of the Sudan in the Arab world.

Coupled with these efforts in the promotion of good relations with its neighbours the Government attempted to promote better relations with the Church organisations. The Catholic and Anglican Churches were approached with a view to obtaining their assistance and support in the repatriation of refugees and their settlement in the Sudan. Representatives of the All Africa Council of Churches were invited to visit the Sudan and the Southern provinces in December 1966. The Government agreed, as a temporary measure until the Missionary Act (1962) could be re-examined, to encourage the employment of African priests and churchmen in the Southern Sudan.

Furthermore, a number of measures on the home front were either implemented or recommended. These recommendations, which arose from the conferences held in the Ministry of Interior in 1966 and 1968 and later approved by the Council of Ministers as a guideline for action, included the encouragement of refugees to return to the Sudan and the establishment of peace villages provided with facilities for education and medical care; the encouragement of visits from outside the Sudan by organisations and individuals known for their willingness to assist in solving the problem; the implementation of more facilities in the South for education, health, communications, etc., and of major economic development schemes, especially in agriculture, forestry, animal health and industry; and the dissemination of knowledge and information on the Southern problem to the outside world and to the Sudanese inside the country with a view to counteracting hostile propaganda.

The most important action, however, was the enactment of a new law — the Amnesty Law of 1967. This provided for an indemnity to unarrested and arrested persons. Under it no legal proceedings would be instituted against any person on account of any act in connection with the mutiny of

18 August 1955. Those who had already been tried and to whom the new Act would not have applied were to be treated leniently and encouraged to apply for the remission of their periods of imprisonment in accordance with Article 16 of the National Constitution.

Not all these recommendations were in fact acted upon, but it cannot be disputed that these findings and recommendations reflected a serious approach, at least by the civil service, towards the solution of the Southern Question. The continuous changes in the government and the instability which continued during 1965–8 did not create good conditions for a peaceful solution of the problem, but the responsibility for this should not be laid at the doorstep of the North. There were other factors at work: the outside world continued to intervene in the problem, and divisions plagued the Southern political movements especially outside the Sudan.

REFERENCES

1. See M. O. Beshir, *op. cit.*, p. 88.
2. Speech by the Prime Minister on the Government's Southern policy, Khartoum 1964.
3. *Ibid*.
4. For a completely opposite view which suggests, unfairly and without evidence, that the military régime was overthrown in order to consolidate the Arab position and speak with one voice against the South, see O. Albino, *op. cit.*, p. 48.
5. *Al Rai Al'am* newspaper, Khartoum, 18 April 1965 and *Vigilant* weekly newspaper, Khartoum, 17 April 1965, quoted by M. A. Salih, *op. cit.*
6. K.N.S., 25 June 1965 quoted by Salih, *op. cit.,* p. 180.
7. K.N.S., 3 November 1966.
8. *Ibid*.
9. Quoted by M. A. Salih, *op. cit.*, p. 189.
10. Proceedings and resolutions of the National Constitution Commission, Khartoum 1967. Also M. A. Salih, *op. cit.*, pp. 229–30.
11. *Ibid*.
12. *Ibid*.
13. M. A. Salih, *op. cit.*, pp. 230–3.
14. *Vigilant*, 24 January 1967.

15. Report by the People's Democratic Party, quoted by Southern Sudan Information Service and *Vigilant*, 12 February 1967.

16. *Al Ayam* newspaper, quoted by *Vigilant* and the Southern Sudan Information Service.

17. Letter from Southern Front to President Obote, quoted in the Southern Sudan Information Service, 8 February 1967.

18. *Ibid.*

19. *Ibid.*

CHAPTER III

ORIGIN AND DEVELOPMENT OF SOUTHERN POLITICAL ORGANISATIONS

The policy of the Condominium administration regarding relations between the Northern and Southern Sudan — which came to be known as the Southern policy,[1] and which was based on separate and different paths of development for the North and the South — had led to a delay in the rise and development of political movements in the South, relative to the North. The lagging behind in the economic and educational fields, the paternalistic attitude of the British administrators and their discouragement of Southern contact with the North were factors in this delayed political development. Contrary to what had been suggested,[2] there was resistance to British administration in the South as well as the North. The character of the resistance may have been different; however, neither the Northerners nor the Southerners acquiesced in alien administration.[3] The influence of earlier Sudanese history and the Southern policy prevented the resistance movements in the two regions from uniting. Even when the 1924 Revolution broke out, and although many of its leaders were officers of 'black' origin and certain parts of the South were the field for the revolution, there was no participation and involvement from the South.

The task of criticizing the Southern policy was undertaken by the Northern nationalists organised in the Graduates Congress. The nationalists opposed the Southern policy because of its future effects and its implication of separate development. Hence their demands in 1939 and 1942 for the removal of restrictions on Northern traders, the expansion of educational facilities, the unification of the educational system and the cancellation of financial aid to missionary schools. The Graduates Congress had its own committees in Juba, Malakal and Wau, but hardly any Southerners participated in the activities of these committees. The activities of the Graduates Congress in the South were limited to the establishment of a mosque in Juba and a few Koranic schools. The only grievance which the Graduates Congress attempted to take up with the Government was the case of Isa Ahmed Fartak, the Sultan of the Feruge tribe, who opposed the missionary education among his Muslim tribesmen, and was dismissed from office and detained in Yez by order of the Governor-General. However, the British administration was able to keep the issue away from the press and from the Graduates Congress.

Political consciousness in the South remained weak, and when it expressed itself in the early 1940s it was in the form of small groups of friends organising themselves in informal political societies, such as Faustino Roro's Southern Sudan Social and Political Association, based in Juba, and Buth Diu's Upper Nile Political Association in Malakal.[4] In 1947 the Southern Officials Welfare Committee was formed. Its membership consisted of Southern civil servants and policemen, and its primary concern was with wages and salaries. The Welfare Committee was able after a successful strike to improve the salaries of its members and the wages of Southern labourers.[5]

This first period of informal social association and embryonic economic and political organisations ended in 1947 – the year of the Juba Conference. The importance of the Juba Conference lay in the fact that it was the first meeting in which the Northerners and Southerners had met together to discuss the future constitutional and administrative relationship between North and South. In addition, it was the first occasion when Southerners from the three provinces had been consulted as a group on this future relationship. It provided the first opportunity for Southern leaders to participate as individuals and jointly as a group in discussing the future of the South in relation to the political and administrative changes in the Sudan.

The discussions of the Conference were political. By participating in them, and in the final decisions, the Southern members were taking the first step in participating in Sudanese politics. Though the Juba Conference 'was unmistakably the beginning of Southern politics'[7] and of the participation of Southern Sudanese in national political affairs, it was not in response to direct political activities in the South. It came as a result of the recommendations of the Sudan Administrative Conference for the establishment of a legislative assembly in which both the North and South would be represented. The members representing the South were selected not on account of the degree of political consciousness they enjoyed, but because they were representatives of the different parts of the South. Nonetheless these members demonstrated a high degree of political insight and sophistication.

The second phase of participation came in December 1948 when thirteen Southerners were appointed to represent the South (out of ninety-five in all, of whom six were British) in the Legislative Assembly. The degree of participation here was much bigger than before. While in the Juba Conference the issue under discussion was relatively simple, the issues in the Legislative Assembly included questions of the future of the Sudan, economic and educational development, and legislative matters. Their concern was no longer limited to the South only but to the whole Sudan.

The logical result of this wider participation and involvement was the increase in political activity not only among the Southern members of the Legislative Assembly but also among those outside it, especially the educated. In 1951 the first political organisation – the Southern Party – was formed in Juba, having been founded by Abdel Rahman Sule, Stanislaus Paysama and Buth Diu. In 1952 a political committee was set up in Juba by Hilary Paul Logali to direct political work, but it did not live long. In 1954, the Southern Party changed its name to the Liberal Party with Benjamin Lwoke as President, Stanislaus Paysama as Vice-President and Buth Diu as General Secretary. Abdel Rahman Sule was responsible for the Juba branch of the party. The Liberal Party functioned as the only political organisation in the South until 1958 when it was dissolved, with all other political parties, by the military régime of General Abboud.

The central point in the Liberal Party's programme was federation, and to this end its leadership based its alliances with the then major political parties of the North: the Umma and the National Unionist Party. The Liberal Party devoted all its energies to obtaining a federal status for the South. It succeeded on 19 December 1955 in persuading Parliament, when making its historical resolution to declare the independence of the Sudan on 1 January 1956, to pass another resolution to the effect that the demand for federation would be given full consideration. In order to fulfil this aim and to serve the immediate demands of the South, the Liberal Party entered into coalitions with different parties at different times. At one time in 1955 it opposed the Government led by the N.U.P., and both Dak Dei and Bullen Alier, minister in Ismail Al Azhari's Cabinet, left the government to join the Liberal Party. In January 1956 Benjamin Lwoke, Stanislaus Paysama and Buth Diu accepted invitations to serve as ministers with Ismail Al Azhari. Six months later Gordon Ayom, Alfred Burjuk and Benjamin Lwoke became ministers in Abdulla Khalil's government. Stanislaus Paysama and the group supporting him in the Liberal Party formed a parliamentary 'Federal Block', opposing the Umma Party. In 1956 Benjamin Lwoke was removed from the presidency of the party and replaced by Stanislaus Paysama. Earlier Buth Diu was replaced by Alfred Burjuk.

The history of the party during the four years of its existence reflected the history of parliamentary life in the Sudan at the time: it was drawn into the national politics, party alliances and coalition governments which characterised that era. Like other political parties it experienced parliamentary floor crossing, internal divisions and personal quarrels, but all this sharpened political interest in the South and among Southerners in the North. Politics in the South, wrote John Howell, 'had a recognisably modern form. M.P.s courted their constituents; parties tried to recruit promising local vote-gatherers as candidates; chiefs, *kujurs* elders found candidates looking for their support. It became a fascinating exercise in the spread of politics if not of political ideas'.[8] The era of Southern involvement in national politics took an upward trend, and in 1958, when new elections were held, there was disillusionment with the old politicians. The 1958 elections brought to parliament a new type of Southern politician: young, better educated and militant in his demand for federation. Men like Joseph Oduhu, Elia Lupe, Luigi Adwok, Daniel Jume and Ezboni Mondiri stood in contrast to many of the old Southern parliamentarians. Inside parliament they joined the Federal Block of Stanislaus Paysama.

The participation and involvement of Southern politicians in national politics continued until November 1958 when the military régime of General Abboud ended parliamentary life, and thus Southern public and direct participation in the political life of the country. The Liberal Party, together with the other political parties in the North, was dissolved. However, the phase which came to an end in November 1958 had witnessed one of the most important events in the North-South relationship and in the process of participation and involvement.

The mutiny of the Equatoria Corps on 18 August 1955 was a reaction against the indifference of the Northern political parties to the demands made by the Southern political leadership for federation, sometimes amounting to outright rejection. The results of the Sudanization policy were disappointing to educated Southerners and were the direct reason for the mutiny. The way the mutiny broke out and the way it was suppressed marked the beginning of the use of force to solve the problems of relations between the North and the South. Until then the problem had been left to the politicians to debate. For the first time since 1924 the 'soldier' became directly involved and active in the field which had hitherto been considered the domain of politicians.

The origins and causes of the mutiny have been recounted in detail in the Cotran Report.[9] We shall be concerned here with those aspects of the mutiny which related to participation, involvement and effects on the development of Southern political organisations. The breakout of the mutiny had not been unexpected. In February 1955 the Governor of Upper Nile province wrote to the Under-Secretary of the Ministry of Interior that the security position was unsatisfactory, and suggested sending Northern troops to be stationed in Malakal. The army authorities did not agree to the proposal on the grounds that such action would affect the morale of the soldiers in the Equatoria Corps. Instead the army authorities proposed the recruitment of a company to be composed of Dinka and Nuer tribesmen, but this was rejected by the civil authorities as impractical, as it could not provide the security needed.

The disagreements between the civil and military authorities in the South at this time arose out of rivalry between them; some of the military men looked at proposals made by the civilians as interference in their area of competence. It would be fair to suggest that co-operation between the civil and military authorities at the provincial levels was well below what was required in the interests of security.

The Equatoria Corps at the time consisted of forty officers, thirty-two of whom were Northerners, and 1,700 N.C.O.s and privates, all Southerners except for a few Northerners in the Signals and Engineering divisions. The commander of the troops, Ismail Salim, was a Northerner, as were all the officers commanding the different areas and companies. These troops were stationed in East Equatoria (Torit, Kapoeta and Luili), West Equatoria (Juba, Yambio and Yei). Upper Nile (Malakal) and Bahr el Ghazal (Wau).

The Anzara events on 25 and 26 July 1955 which led to the use of troops to disperse the riots, and the Torit event of the 7 August 1955 when an attempt was made to murder a Northern soldier, were the first clear indications of the events to come. Although the plan for the mutiny was discovered on 7 August 1955 in the house of Saturlino[7] one of the leaders of the mutiny, no immediate action was taken.

The documents found in Saturlino's home and the investigations carried out later revealed that the plan for the mutiny was made at meetings held in Juba attended by some politicians and parliamentarians of the Liberal Party, and by officers and N.C.O.s from the Equatoria Corps. The politicians involved in the planning were Daniel Jume, Marko Rume, M.P., Secretary of the Liberal Party Committee in Juba, and Benjamin Odimiang, the Liberal Party representative in Torit. The officers and N.C.O.s involved in the planning and execution of the mutiny were Ladingo Renaldo,

Taffeng, Ali Batala, Albino and Saturlino. These were the spear-head of the movement and its organisation among the soldiers.

The plan was to be carried out on the 3 August 1955 but was postponed to 18 August. By 23 August, the mutineers were able to control the whole of Equatoria Province except for Juba. In Bahr el Ghazal the civil and military authorities, assisted by Santino Deng, were able to exclude the mutineers and assume the responsibility for the province when the Governor, the commander of the troops and the senior civil servants left. The troops in Wau were under the command of 2nd-Lieut. Nyang Diu and in Rumbek under 2nd-Lieut. Amin Nimir, the only Northern officer who remained behind. The mutineers had less success in Upper Nile, and the civil and military authorities remained in control. The mutineers received much support in Equatoria province and many Northerners lost their lives, as did many Southerners.

The South was thrown into chaos. The Khartoum authorities acted immediately, declaring a state of emergency. The Governor-General returned from abroad. Troops were sent from the North, and the mutineers were contacted and asked to surrender. They agreed to do so on condition that their surrender would be made to the British troops. When they found that this was impossible, they agreed to surrender just the same. The arrangements for surrender were supervised on the side of the mutineers by 2nd-Lieut. Rinaldo, and by the middle of September 1955, 935 officers, N.C.O.s and men had surrendered with a large quantity of arms and ammunition. In May 1956 the number which had refused to surrender was estimated at 434 with a very large quantity of arms and ammunition. Those who did not surrender either fled to neighbouring countries or disappeared into the countryside with their arms. Military operations against these continued in the following years.

The mutiny had resulted from fear, suspicion and past policies aimed at the creation of a constitutional collapse which, in the case of federation not being granted, would lead ultimately to the separation of the South. Although this was not achieved at the time, the mutiny introduced a new factor in North-South relations: the use of violence and direct involvement of the military on both sides in the Southern Sudan problem.

The policy of the Abboud régime and its attitude towards the South led many Southerners, especially students, politicians, administrators and ex-M.P.s afraid of being arrested, to flee the country in 1960. Those who fled the country included Father Saturnino Lohure, Joseph Oduho and William Deng. As their numbers increased outside the Sudan, they started to organise themselves. In 1962 they created in Leopoldville, Congo, the Sudan African Closed Districts National Union (S.A.C.D.N.U.) with Joseph Oduhu as President, Marko Rume as Vice-President, William Deng as General Secretary and Aggrey Jaden as Deputy General Secretary. Members included Father Saturnino Lohure, Ferdinand Adyang, James Wek Achian, Pancrasio Ocheng, Alexis Mbali, Philip Pedak, Bazia Renzi, Nathaniel Oyet and Valeridio Oregat. In 1963 the name was changed to the Sudan African National Union (S.A.N.U.); its headquarters were in Kampala, Uganda. From then on S.A.N.U. began to seek and organise support inside and outside the Sudan. Its activities outside the Sudan included petitioning the United Nations, the O.A.U., the African Liberation Committee in Dar es Salaam and the Commission of the O.A.U. for Refugees. In all these petitions S.A.N.U. explained the plight of the Southern Sudan and demanded the formation of an international body to investigate the problem. In addition, S.A.N.U. supplied information to journalists and organisations and sought to obtain assistance for the refugees and for its work. Inside the Sudan, S.A.N.U. was receiving support from educated Southerners. 'Since 1962, educated Southerners, many in Government Service, had been forming small cells which passed on information and collected subscriptions for the movement outside.'[10]

Meanwhile, the various groups of former soldiers and policemen who had been living in the bush since the 1955 mutiny continued to attack army and police posts from time to time, but they lacked organisation and leadership. In 1963 these groups joined together under the name of Anya Nya and became the armed wing of S.A.N.U. The claim of some leaders at the time that there was no relation between S.A.N.U.

and the Anya Nya was nothing more than whitewash.[11]

According to McCall[12] the expression Anya Nya is a Latuka corruption of *Inya Nye*, which means literally 'snake venom' or 'incurable poison' in the Moru and Madi languages. The name had powerful associations among the Latuka and Acholi people because of an outbreak of *Inye Nye* poisoning by Madi witches in Opari District during the 1930s. The aims of the Anya Nya were stated in a leaflet in the following words:[13] 'Our patience has now come to an end and we are convinced that only use of force will bring a decision. . . . From today onwards we shall take action . . . for better or worse. . . . We do not want mercy and we are not prepared to give it.'

Their first action was in September 1963 when a police and army post at Pachola on the Ethiopian border was attacked. Attacks then followed on Lasu, Kaya, Kajo-Kaji, Nimule, Katire and other places. In 1964, Father Saturnino was able to obtain arms through the Congo, and this enabled the Anya Nya to spread their activities to Bahr el Ghazal.[14] An attempt was made to capture Wau, but it failed.[15] In 1965 they were able to capture some of the arms and military equipment sent by Egypt and Algeria through the Southern Sudan to the defeated Congolese rebels under Christopher Gbeng, and this enabled them to intensify their activities.

By the end of 1964, the Southern political movement consisted of S.A.N.U. with its military wing, the Anya Nya, and an underground organisation in the Sudan. The latter emerged in October 1964 as the Southern Front with first Gordon Abiei and then Clement Mboro as its President, with Gordon Muortat Mayen as Vice-President and Hilary Paul Logali as Secretary-General.

The Southern Front, which was at first the front of S.A.N.U. inside the Sudan, continued to be the only mouthpiece of the South until the decision of William Deng to return to the Sudan with his breakaway group of S.A.N.U. in 1965, and the appearance in the same year of other groupings such as the Sudan Unity Party led by Santino Deng, the Free Southern Front led by Buth Diu and the Sudan African Socialist Union led by Joseph Garang.

Supporters of S.A.N.U. who had remained outside the
Sudan were going through a difficult period characterised by
conflicts and divisions. They formed a number of groups and
organisations, which although they were agreed on separation
and advocated it, fought and opposed each other. Examples
of these were the Fashoda National Provisional Government,
the African Liberation Front and the Sudan African Freedom
Fighters. In June 1965 the Azania Liberation Front (A.L.F.)
was formed. Its leadership consisted of Joseph Oduhu,
George Kwanai, Pancrasio Ocheng, Father Saturnino Lohure
and Marko Rume; Aggrey Jaden, who was left out, formed
the Sudan African Liberation Front (S.A.L.F.). A reconciliation between these two groups occurred in December 1965
and the name Azania Liberation Front (A.L.F.) was adopted
with Joseph Oduhu as President and Aggrey Jaden as
Vice-President. The other office-bearers were Ezboni Mondiri
(Defence), Elia Lupe (Interior), Philip Pedak (Foreign Affairs), Ibrahim Kao (Justice), Dr. Clement Khamis (Health),
Romano Hassan (Agriculture), L. Wani (Education), Marko
Rume (Refugees) and Ahmed Morgan (Organisation and
co-ordination). The programme of the A.L.F. adopted the
following points as the centre of their policies:

(*a*) The creation of a common nationality and a common
language for the tribes in the South. Consideration should
be given to the development of the pidgin Arabic spoken
in the South as the language of conversation.
(*b*) The promotion of education and literacy in the
liberated areas of the South.
(*c*) The promotion of self-reliance and dependence on the
movement's own resources. In the case of aid received from
outside, this should be without any strings attached to it.
(*d*) Independence from international blocks and no political commitment to any. Co-operation with African states,
especially with the French-speaking countries and the
English-speaking East African countries, particularly Tanzania. Special efforts to be made to promote relations with
Nigeria.

The adoption and declaration of this programme by the
different groups was followed by the visits of Ezboni Mondiri

and Joseph Oduhu to a number of African countries with a view to obtaining their assistance. The programme was given wide publicity in East Africa and the Southern Sudan.

In March 1966 there were further conflicts and divisions within the A.L.F. Joseph Oduhu had earlier dismissed Ezboni Mondiri and Elia Lupe from the A.L.F.'s political bureau and appointed George Kwanai as Vice-President in place of Aggrey Jaden. This action was opposed by the other groups, especially those from Western Equatoria. Oduhu had been accused of tribalism and the promotion of his own friends; also of using aid and assistance received from outside for his own interests.

In August 1967 a large meeting of Southern political leaders outside the Sudan was held in secret at Angudri, between Meridi and Yei near the Congo border, at which it was decided to dissolve all political groups and organisations and establish the Southern Sudan Provisional Government (S.S.P.G.) with headquarters at a place with the code name 'Bongo' on the Juba-Yei road. Aggrey Jaden was appointed President and a political bureau was formed, consisting of Aggrey Jaden, Camelio Dhol Kwat (Vice-President), Francis Mayer (Attorney-General), and Safarino Foly (Minister of Presidential Affairs). In addition, an Executive Council was formed with the following members: Aggrey Jaden – Prime Minister, Akot Ateim – Defence, Elia Lupe – Interior, Gordon Mortat Mayen – Foreign Affairs, Othwan Dak – Education, Gabriel Kao – Justice, George Kwanai – Information, Lawrence Wol – Agriculture, Joseph Oduhu – Communications, Elia Deng – Animal and Natural Resources, David Kwak – Social Affairs and Refugees, and Tadio Pedit – Finance and Economics.

The following were appointed deputy ministers: Camelio Dhol Kwat (Presidential Affairs), Arkangel Kwanji (Defence), Solomon Deng (Interior), Clement Mozi (Foreign Affairs), Andolf Lwat (Education), Daniel Kwot (Finance), Andrew Yak (Information), Lazo Ladjor (Health), Marko Rume (Agriculture), Stephen Lam (Communication), Simon Mobis (Animal and Natural Resources) and Amedo Awad Mohamed (Social Affairs and Refugees).

For the first time the S.S.P.G. had brought within one organisation the different political groups and personalities active in the Southern Sudan question outside the country; as such, this was a step forward towards reconciliation among the different groups. The S.S.P.G. was a 'government' in exile with a political bureau and a council of ministers and deputy ministers.

Its programme was no different from that of the A.L.F. except for the details of the programme which were later worked out. Its policy statements issued in circulars immediately afterwards, which were signed by Aggrey Jaden, included the following points:

1. *National Unity*
(*a*) The S.S.P.G.'s task was to promote national unity between the Southerners and oppose tribal and party divisions. It would consist of representatives of all the three provinces.
(*b*) The S.S.P.G. would send its representatives to the South to explain its policy and persuade the Southern political and tribal leaders that it was the only 'government' that represented them.
(*c*) The South would be united both politically and militarily under a 'president'.
2. *The Constitution*
The S.S.P.G. Constitution would be based on the principle of liberating the South from Arab rule and the only way for the independence of the South would be by means of a military struggle.
3. *The Headquarters of the Government*
The S.S.P.G. would have its own headquarters in the South with representatives and offices inside and outside Africa.
4. *Broadcasting*
There would be a special S.S.P.G. broadcasting service, which would disseminate information about the South to Africa and the rest of the world which would emphasise atrocities by the Arabs, the military successes of the fighters, and other points.
5. *Laws and Regulations*
The S.S.P.G. would issue laws, and regulations defining the duties and functions of the different government officers.
6. *Commander of the Armed Forces*
The Commander of the Army or his representative would be a member of the Council of Ministers.

7. *Ministers and/or Secretaries*
To be selected in accordance with their abilities and experience.

8. *The Oath*
The Ministers would make an oath of loyalty to the S.S.P.G. on their appointment.

9. *The Armed Forces*
(*a*) *A Defence Council* would be constituted from the following: the President, Vice-President, Minister of Defence, Minister of the Interior, Minister of Finance, Commander of the Armed Forces, Chief of Staff and area commanders. The function of the Council was to plan and supervise military operations.

(*b*) *Arms and military equipment.* The first duty of the S.S.P.G. was to procure arms and military equipment, military support and financial and political assistance from other countries.

(*c*) *Supplies.* The S.S.P.G. would negotiate with neighbouring countries the routes and means by which the supplies would be brought into the South.

(*d*) *Administration of the Army.* The administration of the affairs of the armed forces and the promotions of the officers and the men should be the sole responsibility of the commanders of the army. The President and the Minister of Defence should be informed about these promotions.

(*e*) Laws and regulations relative to the administration of the Army would be issued. If necessary an expert should be engaged to advise and help.

(*f*) *The National Army.* The Anya Nya forces would consist of

    (i) a regular army;
    (ii) a guerrilla force.

Six or more military advisers from friendly countries would be appointed to train the regular forces, which should be recruited from among the citizens of the three Southern provinces. The guerrilla forces should be trained at the headquarters of the national army, and should be recruited from the provinces in which they are operating.

(*g*) *National Militia or Guard.* A national militia or guard would be created for the protection of villages and the establishment of law and order.

(*h*) *Special Military Units.* Special army units for intelligence, sabotage, signals and medical services would be established. The intelligence and sabotage units would receive full training.

(*i*) *Scholarships for Military Training.* The scholarships for the training of officers and students were to be discussed with friendly countries. Southern students to be trained abroad should be selected from among those who had completed their secondary education.

10. *Finance*

(*a*) A financial committee under the chairmanship of the President of the S.S.P.G. and the vice-chairmanship of the Minister of Finance would be created. The Committee would be responsible for the administration of all financial matters including the revenue, taxes and assistance from abroad.

(*b*) *Auditing.* Qualified auditors should be appointed.

(*c*) *Budget.* The budget would be divided into two parts – military and civil. The military part should constitute 75 per cent of the whole, and should be supervised by a military finance committee, presided over by the Minister of Defence. The auditors should also audit the military accounts.

(*d*) *Revenue.* The revenue of the S.S.P.G. would be derived mainly from the South. Each province should pay an annual tax assessed on its resources. Other items of revenue would include the selling of ivory and cattle.

(*e*) *Co-operative Societies.* The S.S.P.G. would establish a co-operative society for the marketing of agricultural products, ivory, cattle, etc.

(*f*) *Agriculture.* The population would be encouraged to increase agricultural production so as to increase the revenue of the S.S.P.G.

Another statement signed by Camelio Dhol Kwat, the Vice-President, listed the functions and duties of the different ministries in the S.S.P.G.:

Ministry of Defence. To be responsible for the organisation of the Anya Nya in a united army, the training of the Anya Nya and the appointment of military advisers from outside. In addition, to be responsible for the formulation of military laws and regulations for the approval of the Council of Ministers.

Ministry of Interior. To be responsible for the organisation and administration of local government, the formulation of laws and regulations for that purpose, the training of administrators and local government officers abroad and the creation of a small armed police force to assist the armed forces and the militia.

Ministry of Foreign Affairs. To be responsible for the promotion of relations with foreign countries, liaison with foreign countries through S.S.P.G. representatives and disseminating information on the Southern Sudan problem.

Ministry of Animal and Natural Resources. To be responsible for the appointment of qualified veterinary officers, the protection of wild animal life, the organisation and marketing of cattle and hides, and the training of veterinary officers. In addition, to be responsible for the development of the country's mineral wealth and the appointment of experts for this purpose.

Ministry of Health. To be responsible for the establishment of mobile health units for the treatment of the Anya Nya and government officers, the appointment and training of medical and public health officers and nurses and obtaining medical equipment.

Ministry of Justice. To be responsible for justice in the South. The Chief Justice and Attorney-General to be responsible to the Minister of Justice. The Ministry to establish State Courts and Native Courts.

Ministry of Education. To be responsible for the education of Southerners in the South, among the refugees and those abroad. For this purpose to establish mobile schools, organise adult education centres and the training of teachers.

Ministry of Information. To be responsible for the promotion of good relations between the Government and the population, and for information and propaganda outside the South. For this purpose, to establish a broadcasting service, newspapers, bulletins, etc.

Ministry of Communications. To be responsible for the communication of information between the different military and civil units, and between the South and the outside world. For this purpose to train Southerners and establish radio stations and a postal service.

Ministry of Social Affairs and Refugees. To be responsible for the social and community development and services in the South and among the refugees, the establishment of clubs and centres and the collection of information on the Southerners resident in the North. Also to be responsible for communication on refugee problems with international and voluntary organisations operating in the field of refugees.

Ministry of Presidential Affairs. To be responsible for the administration and co-ordination of the work of the Council of Ministers, the movement of ministers and the preparation of the agenda of meetings of the Council of Ministers.

For the purpose of administration, the South was divided into three provinces, corresponding to the existing province boundaries, nine regions and twenty-two districts. According to the plan, each province was to have its own province commissioners, regional commissioners and district commissioners appointed to each unit. The provinces were to be administered by a province council consisting of elected representatives from the regional councils and the heads of departments. The chairman, the vice-chairman and secretary of the councils were to be elected from among the members elected to the Council. In addition, an executive council consisting of the heads of departments and presided over by the province commissioner would be established.

The regions were to have their own councils and executive councils. The regional council, like the provincial council, would consist of representatives from the elected members from the district councils and the heads of departments at regional level. The regional executive council was to consist of the regional heads of departments and elect its own chairman and secretary. The functions of the regional council would include the collection of taxes, the administration of health services, supervision of elementary education and the making of laws relevant to the region.

The district council was to consist of elected members from the local councils and the heads of departments at the district level. The district commissioner was the chairman of the council and the administrative officer was its secretary. Like the regional council, its function included the collection of taxes, health and educational services, and local roads.

The tribal chiefs were recognized as the representatives of the administration in the rural areas.

Each province, region and district was designated a specified number of accountants, cashiers, etc.

Equatoria Province was divided into the Eastern region (consisting of Kapoeta and Torit Districts) the Central region (consisting of Juba, Yei and Amadi districts), and the Western region (consisting of Yambio and Meridi districts). Bahr el Ghazal province was divided into the Aweil/Raja region (consisting of Aweil and Raja districts), the Jur River region (consisting of Rumbek and Tonj districts), Upper Nile province was divided into the Nile Basin region (consisting of Bor, Fanjak, Bentiu districts), the Sobat Valley region (consisting of the Nasir, Akobo and Pibor districts) and the Northern region (consisting of Malakal, Kodok and Renk districts). This organisation was hardly put into operation except for the appointment of Pancrasio Ocheng, Daniel Jume, Izbon Goode, Solaman Yak, Antipas Ayol and Massio Opul as commissioners for the regions. Their duty was to implement the administrative structure and establish an administration in the areas controlled by the Anya Nya.

In addition, a defence committee was established for each of the three provinces. Aggrey Jaden, George Kwanai, and Lawrence Wol were appointed chairmen of the Equatoria, Upper Nile and Bahr el Ghazal defence committees respectively; they were made responsible for the formation of the committees, whose functions included the organisation and unification of the Anya Nya forces, the planning and direction of military operations, the supply of arms and ammunition to the Anya Nya and the obtaining of funds and assistance for the S.S.P.G.

A programme on foreign policy issued by the S.S.P.G. included new policies not included in the previous policy statements and declaration. The new policy points were: (a) co-operation with all the national liberation movements in Africa for the liberation of the Southern Sudan; (b) opposition to imperialism, communism and tribalism; (c) support for the International Peace Movement; (d) support for the creation of the East African Common Market; (e) opposition to religious or racial prejudices and discrimination among the members and supporters of the S.S.P.G., and with this understanding a desire to negotiate and co-operate with any Arab government.

Thus for the first time could be seen an attitude of

reconciliation with the Arab governments who showed willingness to listen and discuss the Southern problem. Again there was a desire to co-operate with the 'Peace Movement', while at the same time being anti-communist. Imperialism, communism and tribalism were all lumped together and became targets of opposition by the movement. The only explanation of these contradictions was that the programme, by being written in this way, was intended to satisfy the different elements and different political groups which had emerged inside the movement during the previous years. The need for unity was such that it was necessary to draw up a programme in which all groups would be accommodated, irrespective of their ultimate aims and objectives.

Besides these statements and policies, a part of which was carried out, the most important development was the appeal to all Southerners living outside to return to the South and participate in the military and political work of the S.S.P.G. and the Anya Nya, and to Southerners living inside the Sudan not to co-operate with the so-called 'Arab' Government of the North. Not only that but the appeal condemned any Southern party working inside the Sudan and declared that the S.S.P.G. would not recognise such parties as in any way representing Southern views or any part of them.

According to the appeal, the S.S.P.G. was the only legitimate party and government of the South. It was in fact condemning both S.A.N.U. and the Southern Front for their participation in the political developments inside the Sudan, including parliamentary elections, and for holding ministerial posts. S.A.N.U. under the leadership of Deng was naturally opposed, and looked upon as no more than a group 'of young adventurers who passed as intellectuals'.[1][7]

The Southern Front, which had enjoyed good relations with the groups outside and reflected their thinking, was no longer in their favour. The S.S.P.G. set out to promote a policy on non-co-operation and non-reconciliation with the North. But in its programme, policies, and activities the S.S.P.G. clearly tried to please too many elements at once. The result was the appearance of tribal and personal rivalries. Disagreements among the leaders progressively emerged and divided the movement.

By September 1968, 'Jaden felt that he was not being respected and supported in his leadership. He began to take a cautious and reserved attitude to the issues. It was alleged that there was an underground movement to depose him, championed by his Vice-President, Camelio Dhol. The situation became confused as tribalism entered the struggle for power, and Jaden abdicated his position and fled to Nairobi'.[18] A convention was held in March 1969 at Balgo-Bindi near Yei under the chairmanship of Camelio Dhol Kwat. The S.S.P.G. was replaced by the Nile Provisional Government with Gordon Mortat Mayen as President.

Mayen had previously been the President of the Southern Front and attended the Round Table Conference. In 1965 he replaced Ezboni Mondiri as Minister of Communications when the latter was dismissed from the Transitional Government. He left the country in 1968 and became active in the political movement and among the Anya Nya. His Nile Provisional Government was dominated by the Dinka and had a cabinet of eight ministers of whom four were Dinka, two Nuer, one Gor and one Bari. This did not please Aggrey Jaden and his supporters, who were mainly from Equatoria province. They therefore opposed the Nile Provisional Government (N.P.G.) from the beginning.

The programme of the N.P.G. did not differ from that of the S.S.P.G., which was the establishment of an independent separate state in the South through military action and in co-operation with the Anya Nya. The N.P.G. declared that since it was fighting the Arabs of the North, it would co-operate with all those who supported its programme and political aims. However, divisions and disagreements soon appeared among its supporters. The Sudan Azania Organisation under Ezboni Mondiri and the Sue River Republic Organisation appeared. This added to the existing confusion.

In July 1969, General Taffeng declared his opposition to the Nile Provisional Government and formed the Anyidi State Government. He ordered the N.P.G. to be dissolved and declared his opposition to all the other groups trying to obtain the support of the Anya Nya. A statement issued by the Anyidi State Government summed up Taffeng's attitude towards the politicians:

For nearly seven years since Southern Sudanese Africans began their campaign against Arab domination, very little has been achieved. To leave things to proceed would mean a sell-out of the Southern people as a whole . . . politicians were found to be incapable of informing the world outside about the movement.[19]

An Anyidi Revolutionary Council was formed from the following: Major-General Taffeng (Chairman); Brigadier Paul Ali Batala (Vice-Chairman); and the following were members: Colonel David Dada, Colonel Paul Nygory, Captain Emanual Euor, Captain Sunday Jean, Captain Hybok Suru, Aggrey Jaden, Akot Ateim, Elia Lupe, Camelio Dhol, Amedo Awad Mohamed, and Gabriel Wani.

The Council of Ministers was formed as follows: Major General Taffeng (Prime Minister), Brigadier Paul Ali Batala (Deputy Prime Minister), Aggrey Jaden (Foreign Minister), Akot Ateim (Interior), Eliaba Surur (Finance), Colonel Frederick Maggot (Defence), Elia Lupe (Justice), Rev. Paul Puot (Education), Camelio Dhol Kwat (Animal Resources), Samuel Abu John (Health), Joseph Oduhu (Information), Colonel Joseph Lagu (Communications and Planning), Arkangelo Wani (Industry and Mining), and Michael Pauli (State Affairs). It can be seen that the Anyidi State Government included all the groups except that of Gordon Muortat Mayen, President of the N.P.G., and his close supporters.

The Anyidi State Government set out to consolidate military and civil administration in the areas which it controlled. It established its headquarters at Mortu near the Sudan-Uganda border. Military camps were set up at Owing Kibul, Atto, Idali, Abba and Kabish. Most of these camps were near the Sudan's borders with Uganda, Congo and Ethiopia, and some incorporated strips and stores. It was reported that arms and military equipment were being received in large quantities across the borders with Uganda, Congo, Ethiopia and the Central African Republic or dropped by aeroplanes. Contacts with churches and voluntary organisations in Italy, France, the U.S.A., West Germany and Britain were stepped up. On the military side the emphasis of the Anyidi State Government was on guerrilla activity, especially near the Sudan borders, and on the promotion of attacks on towns and military and police posts in the South. The plan would then be to move into the next stage of organising a conventional army.

However, the same divisive forces which had led to the discontinuation of the previous political organisations and provisional governments soon appeared: tribalism, personal rivalries and disagreements over the distribution of foreign assistance and aid. General Taffeng, who was critical of all politicians, was blamed for including some of these in his government of the Anyidi State. It was felt that he was too old to cope with the changes taking place inside the Sudan and the Southern political movement.

The Southern politicians outside the Sudan were described by Dunstan M. Wai as

> confused and [having] lost contact with the real issues involved in the North-South conflict. Some of them have no keen interest in the Anya-Nya and have even worked for the disunity of the Anya-Nya to serve their own interests. Sheer personal ambition has led to power struggles resulting in internal divisions, thereby creating a meaningless government purporting to represent the Southern Sudanese. Incompetence and lack of political foresight are common among them. They have refused to see the fact that they lack the ability to put political issues in proper perspective and have assumed certain positions of power which they are unable to shoulder. All these factions suffer from the lack of a serious intention to serve the people they claim to lead, and egoistic pursuits occupy much of their time. The creation of a multiplicity of presidents was motivated by the struggle for financial help from their benefactors. Tribalism has also plagued all Southern politicians outside the Sudan. I have already indicated that the formation of the Anyidi Revolutionary Government was basically tribally motivated and aimed at countering the Dinka dominance in the Nile Government. Another common element among them is that they fall under the category of ignorant élites.[20]

He also accused them of 'blackmailing and exploiting the Southern masses',[21] to 'have failed to understand the complex operation of the machinery of Cold War politics',[22] and to have contacts with 'some imperialist agents'.[23]

In July 1970, Colonel Joseph Lagu, Eastern commander of the Anya Nya forces, revolted against Taffeng and declared the formation of the Southern Sudan Liberation Movement. 'Colonel Lagu', wrote Dunstan M. Wai, 'gained ground and eventually united all the Anya Nya officers under his command, pensioned off General Taffeng and declared the Anya Nya as the sole authority in the Southern Sudan. The Nile Provisional Government dissolved itself in mid-1970 in the interests of unity, and subsequently all the rest of the parties followed its example and declared support for Colonel Lagu's leadership'.[24]

Colonel Lagu established the headquarters of his command at Owing Kibul. By eliminating the Southern politicians from the leadership of the Anya Nya, all the power and direction of the Southern political movement was transferred to the military commanders of the Anya Nya. Lagu and his officers became solely responsible for the Southern Sudan Liberation Movement. He did not, however, exclude all the politicians from his movement. Some, like Lawrence Wol and Mading deGarang, continued to work under him, but his emphasis and that of his supporters was on the promotion and intensification of the guerrilla war in the South. More arms and military equipment were brought in from outside. Israeli advisers and mercenaries were engaged and brought into the war.

The aims and policies of the Southern Sudan Liberation Movement under the leadership of Joseph Lagu were explained in a booklet issued to the Anya Nya soldiers in January 1972, one month before the Addis Ababa Agreement. Joseph Lagu writes:

> The goal of our struggle is clear and straightforward — the right of self-determination for our people. We want our people to be able of its own free will and under no threat or fear, to determine its destiny, either to remain in a unitary Sudan as a truly autonomous region, or to have nothing whatsoever to do with the North and tie our future with that of our African brothers in their states on our Southern borders. We shall accept no unity imposed on us by the North nor shall consider any arrangement concluded by Southerners in the service of their Arab

masters. The future of the South can be decided only through a settlement negotiated with the Anya Nya / S.S.L.M.[2][5]

The Anya Nya soldiers were told that their fight was a continuation of the Revolt of the Equatoria Corps in 1955, and that they were fighting to defend the African values of the Southern Sudanese and to bring the tribes of the South Sudan into one national framework. The aims and objectives were summarized in the following terms:[2][6]

WE BELIEVE:
1. That despite the enemy's machinations aimed at dominating our people and colonizing our country, the just struggle that we lead will end victoriously. That our specifically African — as distinct from Arab — identity and the common aspirations which unite all our tribes in a common struggle fully qualify us for nationhood and the right of self-determination.
2. That by rejecting the attempted arabization of Southern Sudan and by adhering to our African identity and heritage we exercise a basic human right which is bound to be recognized by everybody sooner or later.
3. That by waging our own war of Liberation we also block Arab and Russian imperialist expansionism southwards and protect our brothers in East and Central Africa.
4. That if the enemy persists in refusing our just demands we are capable of going on fighting indefinitely and so shall we do — until we win.

This statement is to be compared with another made by Lagu after his return to the Sudan:

'I never was a separatist. I never believed in the secession of the South from the North; I still hold that belief. My only aim was to obtain recognition for Southerners. It was my opinion that such an aim could be achieved through the application of force, but I never intended to use force to achieve separation. I had resorted to force because I concluded that the successive Khartoum Governments were not willing to concede the point.'

Lagu and his group seem to have been successful in building up the Anya Nya forces and their morale. A report

by the Joint Military Commission in October 1972 described
the Anya Nya as follows:[27]

1. *Composition.* The Anya Nya forces were composed of a
headquarters and three brigades.
(*a*) The headquarters and the 1st Brigade, comprising four
battalions organised on a tribal basis, were in Equatoria
province; this was the largest and best armed force.
(*b*) The 2nd Brigade was in Upper Nile province. It was
incompletely organised and also on a tribal basis, tribalism
being particularly dominant in this area.
(*c*) The 3rd Brigade in Bahr el Ghazal province was
composed of three well organised battalions.
2. *Armaments.* Most units were armed with automatic
weapons of Chinese or Belgian makes, light machine-guns
and 'Mark IVs'. They also had anti-aircraft weapons of
12.7 mm bore, mortars of 81 mm. bore and bazookas,
together with large quantities of explosives, including
anti-tank guns and anti-tank mines.
3. *Communications.* There was wireless contact between
the command and the following areas – Yei River, Mundri,
Yambio, Torit, Kapoeta and Angudri – and with headquarters in Upper Nile and Bahr el Ghazal.
4. *Transport.* Movement was mainly on foot, with motor
vehicles at the border areas in order to reach neighbouring
countries.
5. *Uniform.* There was no single uniform, but they had
managed to obtain standardized clothing from East
African markets.
6. *Training.*
(*a*) Discipline was very good with full obedience to
leadership.
(*b*) At company and platoon levels infantry drill was good
and tactics were to a satisfactory standard.
(*c*) Officers' training was as follows:
 (i) Basic training for three months within the area,
 including tactics, drill and use of arms at platoon level.
 (ii) Commando training for six months at headquarters
 including tactics, use of explosives, map-reading and
 judo.
 (iii) Infantry training was done abroad (in Israel) for
 three months preceded by one month's preparation at
 headquarters. Five batches were sent starting in 1969.
 The number of officers having attended such training
 was about 200.

(iv) It was decided to have the same course as that obtained in Israel conducted in the Sudan with the assistance of instructors from abroad. Two batches were trained in this way.

(v) Special courses for the signals, engineers and medical corps were conducted at headquarters. Some officers were sent abroad for training.

The joint military commission included ex-Anya Nya officers It is understood that whenever the word 'abroad' is used, Israel is meant.

Meanwhile, confrontation between the Sudanese army and the Anya Nya continued. One result was that the number of displaced persons and refugees increased. The number displaced inside the country was estimated in 1969 at 150,000. It was estimated in that year that 176,900 Sudanese refugees were living in neighbouring countries, distributed as follows:

Central African Republic	22,900
Ethiopia	20,000
Uganda	74,000
Zaire	60,000
	176,900

The major refugee settlements were at Mboki in the Central African Republic, Gambaila in Ethiopia, Amendi and Kypo in Zaire, and Onigo, Agogo, Acolpii and Nakapupurit in Uganda. Funds amounting to US $8,503,000 were provided by the United Nations High Commissioner for Refugees to provide the essential services for these settlements.

The refugees were not always welcome in the host countries, where they caused economic and social problems. The refugee settlements were often used for recruiting Anya Nya supporters, and became centres for political activity by the Southern political leaders. Arms were freely exchanged. Missionaries known for their hostility to the Sudan, such as McClore, Ferrari and Allan Reed, moved freely in the refugee camps.

The refugee problem, therefore, became an important factor in the Sudan's relations with its neighbours. The containment of the activities of the political leaders, the Anya Nya and those individuals and organisations which supported their cause depended to a large extent on the development of good relations between the Sudan and these countries. Thus at the beginning of 1969 the Southern Sudan problem became part and parcel of Sudanese relations with the outside world, especially with its neighbours.

REFERENCES

1. For a detailed study of the Southern policy, see M. O. Beshir, *op. cit.*, pp. 18–68 and 115–35. Also Abdel Rahim Mudathir, *The Development of British Policy in the Southern Sudan 1899–1947*, Khartoum, 1968.

2. R. S. O'Fahey, *The Southern Sudan: Symposium of Conflicts in the Middle African Region*, International Institute of Strategic Studies, London, 1971.

3. For a detailed study of the resistance movement in the Sudan, see M. O. Beshir, *Revolution and Nationalism in the Sudan*, Rex Collings, London, 1974.

4. John Howell, 'Politics in the Southern Sudan', *African Affairs*, April 1973.

5. *Ibid.*

6. For the Minutes of the Juba Conference see M. O. Beshir *The Southern Sudan, op. cit.*, Appendix 9, pp. 136–53.

7. Howell, *op. cit.*

8. *Ibid.*

9. Sudan Government: Southern Sudan Disturbances, Report of the Commission of Enquiry, Khartoum 1955.

10. Howell, *op. cit.*

11. *The Observer*, London, 6 October 1963 and Beshir, *op. cit.*

12. S. McCall, 'The Rise of a Provisional Government in Southern Sudan' in Social Science Council's Seminar held in the University of East Africa, 9–12 December 1969, mimeographed.

13. *Ibid.*

14. *Ibid.*

15. Beshir, *op. cit.*, p. 84.

16. Howell, *op. cit.*

17. Albino, *op. cit.*, p. 67.

18. D. M. Wai (ed.) *The Southern Sudan: the Problem of National Integration, op. cit.*

19. Personal information.

20. Wai, *op. cit.*, pp. 163–4.

21. *Ibid.*

22. *Ibid.*

23. *Ibid.*

24. *Ibid.*
25. South Sudan Liberation Movement, Anya Nya, 'What we fight for in South Sudan'.
26. *Ibid.*
27. Report of the Joint Military Commission, Khartoum, October 1972, pp. 16–17.

CHAPTER IV

THE MAY REVOLUTION AND THE SOUTHERN PROBLEM

On 25 May 1969 the parliamentary régime was overthrown, the coalition Government led by Mohamed Ahmed Mahjoub was dismissed, the transitional constitution was suspended and a new régime was established – namely the May Revolutionary Government led by Major-General Gaafar Mohamed Nimeiri.

In his first statement to the nation on that date, Nimeiri outlined the reasons which had led him and the other members of the Revolutionary council to take over power, and the failure of previous governments to solve the Southern problem was among those mentioned. On 9 June, after several joint meetings of the Revolutionary Council and the Council of Ministers, a policy statement on the Southern Sudan was announced.[1] It emphasised four points:

1. The Revolution was a continuation of the Revolution of October 1964. The Government had then recognised for the first time that a Southern problem existed, and endeavoured to solve it through the Round Table Conference. However, it had not been given enough time. The new Government of May 1969 was committed to the same objectives as those of the October 1964 Government.

2. All Southerners abroad and at home were called upon to see that peace and stability prevailed in the South, and that life should return to normal conditions so as to enable the new Government to carry out its policy.

3. The need for building a broad socialist-oriented democratic movement in the South as part of the revolutionary structure in the North was an essential pre-requisite for the application of regional autonomy.

4. The Southern people should have the right to develop their respective customs and traditions within a united socialist Sudan.

Regional autonomy was conceived by the new Government as part of the socialist orientation and policies of the régime. Its implementation depended, according to the Government, on the acceptance of what the statement described as the socialist-oriented democratic movement in the South. Regional autonomy was, therefore, closely connected with the growth of a new political movement different from the Southern political movement already existing in the North or South.

Because regional autonomy was seen to be a target to be achieved in the future, after the fulfilment of certain pre-requisites, a programme of action embodying the following points was drawn up:

1. the continuation and further extension of the Amnesty Law;
2. economic, social and cultural development of the South;
3. the appointment of a Minister for Southern Affairs;
4. the training of Southern personnel to shoulder the new responsibilities;
5. the creation of a special economic planning board and the preparation of a special budget for the South.

The declaration and the programme of action were hailed in both the North and the South as the most important single action of the new régime. In the words of a leading Southerner, it was received with more enthusiasm than the overthrow of the military régime of General Abboud in October 1964.[2] In the North too it was viewed as a significant step in the right direction. The appointment of Joseph Garang, a leading Southern Sudanese communist, as Minister for Southern Affairs was a source of assurance since he was known for his support of unity and his opposition to separation.

It should be noted in this context that the Sudan Communist Party was the first to advocate autonomy for the Southern Provinces. As far back as 1954, a statement by the Anti-Imperialist Front (the forerunner of the Sudan Communist Party) published in *Al Saraha* newspaper on 28 September 1954, warned that the Southern problem was an urgent one and that a solution to it should be found so as to avoid complications when independence came. The policy stated that the right of the Southern nationals to establish their own local or autonomous government provided that this would be in a united Sudan, was the key to solving the problem. This view was repeatedly made by the representatives and supporters of the Anti-Imperialist Front inside and outside Parliament during the period 1954–6 and was included in its programme of action published in April 1955. The programme specifically stated that the solution of the problem could only come through the protection of the Southern communities against national oppression and of their right to autonomous rule, and the development of their local laws within a united country taking into consideration the general interests of the country.

These views and policies were later adopted by the Communist Party, which replaced the Anti-Imperialist Front and became the official policy of the party.

Notwithstanding this, some Southerners, especially from among those living outside the Sudan, were hesitant in their support; they were suspicious of the North and were not easy to persuade. They argued that only actual implementation would convince them of the North's seriousness. They did not welcome the appointment of Joseph Garang to carry out the policy; as a communist he was suspect, especially among those who worked closely with the Church.

In pursuance of the new policy the Ministry of Southern Affairs was set up under Joseph Garang. His functions as a deputy Minister were to advise on the best means of carrying out the Southern programme, the supervision and co-ordination of all government activities in the South and the execution of economic and social projects.[3]

The formation of a Ministry for Southern Affairs was welcomed, although it fell short of the expectations of many Southern leaders, who had hoped for a fully fledged and autonomous Ministry for Southern Affairs.[4] It is worth noting here that the idea of establishing a Ministry for Southern Affairs was not new. The Constitutional Commission of 1951, appointed by the Governor-General under the chairmanship of Judge R. C. Stanley-Baker, did consider a proposal to the effect that 'a Ministry for Southern Affairs should be established, headed by a minister who must himself be from the South and whose duty would be to assist the Governor-General in the exercise of his special powers in respect of the South'.[5] According to this proposal, 'the Minister for Southern Affairs would be responsible for promoting in the Council of Ministers and introducing in the Assembly measures for economic and social bettering of the peoples of the South. The Board was to operate in an advisory capacity only and would in no way share the Minister's responsibility'.[6] It would also be the Minister's duty 'to make formal representations to the Governor-General about any pending administrative or legislative measures which in his opinion would adversely affect the interests or the wellbeing of the peoples of the South'.[7] However, this proposal was rejected by the Legislative Assembly. Instead it was agreed, to the dismay and opposition of the Southern members in the Assembly, that at least one member of the Council of Ministers should be from the South.[8]

This proposal has been quoted at length to show that the proposal for establishing a Ministry for Southern Affairs was not new; it had been there since 1951 but no subsequent governments had been far-sighted or courageous enough to carry it out. When the Ministry was created in 1969, it was again felt by some Southerners that it fell short of what they had hoped for, but in spite of this, its creation, and the way in which it had been created, were important and positive steps towards solving the Southern problem. At least an organisation had been established to advise on policies and follow through the implementation of these policies.

A month later, in July 1969, the Minister for Southern Affairs visited Uganda in an attempt to explain the new policy and persuade the reluctant Southern politicians to return home. In August 1969, the Chairman of the Revolutionary Council toured the South to explain the new policy, and emphasised the need for peace and for economic development. He called on the rebel leaders to return to the Sudan and share in the execution of the new policy. In

October 1969 the Amnesty Law of 1967, which was due to
expire in that month, was extended to October 1970; later it
was extended again to October 1971.

The Southern Sudanese were again participating in the
making of national policies, and this had an immediate effect
on the security situation in the South and on the position of
the refugees outside the Sudan. The following figures for the
growth of population in selected towns immediately after the
new policy was declared provide clear evidence of the extent
to which the situation had improved.

	1963	Sept. 1965	Dec. 1969
Juba	18,000	7,000	65,000
Meridi	4,000	29	15,000
Yei	3,000	Nil	8,000
Yambio	2,500	Nil	8,500
Anzara	5,000	200	9,000
Torit	3,000	Nil	11,000
Tombura	2,000	110	15,000

Some of this growth had resulted directly from the new
policy, but the figures for the seven months following the
June declaration were particularly significant since they
showed an increase in the number returning to the towns
near the Sudan-Uganda borders.

RETURNING REFUGEES TO EQUATORIA PROVINCE 1969[9]

	March	April	May	August	September
Yambio	1,160	315	535	33	18
Anzara	—	—	—	59	69
Yei	1,854	1,343	438	126	200
Kapoeta	—	39	—	2,500	2,500
Meridi	1,434	391	1,186	434	703
Torit	61	123	123	105	202
	4,509	2,211	2,262	3,257	3,692

The immediate influx of returning refugees, and the
expected increase in the future, prompted the Government to
seek assistance from international organisations. In December

1969 an agreement was signed with the World Food Programme to supply the Sudan with urgent food aid to the value of $435,000 and another grant of $11,427,000 in 1970.

It was already clear by the end of 1969 that an important obstacle to the implementation of the new policy was the administrative set-up in the Southern provinces: a reform of the administrative machinery was needed if the new policy was to be implemented successfully. The Council of Ministers Resolution No. 111 of 3 December 1969 appointed a ministerial committee to study and recommend ways and means necessary for the implementation of the June Declaration and the policies adopted since. The ministerial committee recommendations were adopted on 24 June 1970 (*vide* Resolution No. 225 of the Council of Ministers). These were:

1. Selection from among the existing officials and employees in all ministries of the most efficient and highly competent cadres, who believe in the scientific solution of the Southern problem, for immediate transfer to the Southern provinces to fill all the approved posts and vacancies on all levels, provincial and district.

2. Application of the policy of transfer to the South promptly and decisively at all levels, thus abandoning the unsound view which considered transfer to the South as a means of punishing unproductive and undesirable elements.

3. The minimum duration of service in the South for all officials and employees to be three years.

4. Selection of trustworthy Southern personnel with devotion to the declared government policy for the South to work in technical ministries such as Health, Animal Resources, Works, Agriculture and Forestry. This selection should be made after consultation with the Minister of State for Southern Affairs.

5. Provision of essential services for the employees working in the South, such as housing and transport.

6. Transfers should be simultaneous in all the ministries and must take place not later than 30 January 1970.

7. Regular inspection tours by ministers, under-secretaries, directors of departments and other high-ranking state offic-

ials of the Southern provinces to facilitate first-hand checks on and knowledge of the process of work, as well as ensuring that the declared policy of the Government is being implemented.

8. Appointment of a deputy or assistant under-secretary by each of the ministries enlisted, to supervise, direct and co-ordinate its departmental activities in the South.

Three deputy or assistant under-secretaries to be immediately transferred to the South to be stationed there, from the following ministries: Agriculture and Forestry, Agricultural Production and Agrarian Reform, Animal Resources, Health, Co-operatives and Rural Development, Education and Instruction, Interior (Police), and National Guidance. These ministries were to delegate and invest in the officials appointed wide discretionary powers to enable them to discharge their responsibility within the limits of the approved budget, and the projects to be implemented in co-ordination with the Minister for Southern Affairs.

The Council of Ministers also decided to establish a co-ordination council and an economic and planning committee. The functions of the co-ordination council were to be

1. General supervision and execution of the general policy in the region.
2. Distribution, co-ordination and implementation of the general budget.
3. To undertake the supervision of any other executive responsibilities within the Region.

The Chairman of the Council was to be the Minister of State for Southern Affairs. Members were to be the Officer Commanding Troops in the South, the Commissioners of Bahr el Ghazal, Equatoria and Upper Nile provinces; the Regional Directors of Agriculture and Forestry, Health, Education, Agricultural Production and Agrarian Reform, Rural Development and Co-operatives, National Guidance, Animal Resources, and Internal Trade and Supply; the Deputy Commissioner of Police (South); The Director, Ministry of Southern Affairs, was to be Secretary.

The Economic and Planning Committee for the South consisted of the heads of departments in the South plus four other persons from outside the civil service. Here again the Minister of State for Southern Affairs was to be Chairman, while the representative of the Ministry of Planning and the Treasury was to be Secretary. The membership of the Economic and Planning Committee was later enlarged to include the Officer Commanding Troops in the South, the three provisional commissioners and the Deputy Commissioner of Police. Provision was made for joint meetings of the Council and the Committee.

This elaborate organisation was not put into practice, and it never functioned. The ministries were reluctant to make the required appointments and transfer those appointed to the South. Some were reluctant to give up their powers to the proposed Council and Economic and Planning Committee. The criticism levelled at the recommendations was their attempt to implement regionalism through an apparatus mainly composed of selected Northern civil servants and administrators. It was argued that according to the recommendations, the Minister of Southern Affairs was no more than a chairman of committees of Northern civil servants, with no power or means to implement any decisions reached by the Co-ordination Council or the Economic and Planning Committee. These two bodies did in fact hold some joint meetings, but little was achieved. The most optimistic Southerners regarded the Resolution by the Council of Ministers as going half way towards implementing the declared policy.[10] The missing half was undoubtedly the more important.

In the same month of January 1970, a sum of £S4 million was appropriated for a crash development programme, mainly for the improvement of animal health, for experimental studies in the growing of sugar cane, tea, coffee and rice, promoting a fish industry, and for the reconstruction and equipment of seven hospitals and of bridges and deep-bore wells.

Abel Alier, the Minister of Supply and Industry, and a leading member of the Southern Front who had played a major role in Southern policies since 1965, visited Uganda in February 1970 with the aim of persuading the Southern politicians that the new Khartoum Government was serious and sincere in its policy towards the South, and that they should be patient and give it a chance. In an address which he delivered at the Students' Guild at Makerere University, he reviewed the steps taken by the Government to implement the new policy in the following words:[11]

'644 Southern policemen have been recruited since the Revolution. Police working in the South were previously recruited in the Northern Sudan, but this has now been changed. Last December, seventeen Southern officer cadets were taken in to the Military College. Compare this with ten recruited between 1959 and January 1969. Recently a special intake of six Southerners has been made to the Police College. The door has been opened for recruitment of Southerners into the Army. This was restricted after the 1955 mutiny and almost prohibited during the military régime of General Abboud. Over 200 men have already been recruited. Three Southerners have recently been appointed to important positions in the armed forces. One is Commandant of Paratroopers; another is Deputy Commandant of the Military College and a third is Commandant of the Officers' Training School. In the police, the Deputy Commandant of Police in Equatoria province is a Southerner, and the Commandant of Police and one of his deputies in the Upper Nile province are Southerners. These appointments were made a few months after the Revolution. Appointments, promotions and transfers of Southerners in civil administration will come out shortly.

'An economic planning board is being appointed. Its members will have their headquarters in Juba where also a new nucleus of administration for the South will be established at the end of February.

'Southerners have been appointed recently to three Provincial Councils in Malakal, Juba and Wau. Their task is to assist in the running of provincial affairs. It is for them to prove their worth once entrusted with this responsibility.

'A third senior secondary school for boys has recently been opened in Malakal. The headmaster of the school is a Southerner from Nimule. He is the first Southerner ever to be appointed to this status.

'A Medical Assistant School that was closed since 1955

is now being re-opened in Juba. Its principal is a Southerner.

'A department for Christian Affairs has been set up in the Ministry of Education. Two prominent Christian leaders, a Catholic and a Protestant, have been appointed to this office. Up to the time of the Revolution only one department of Religious Affairs existed. It was exclusively for the Muslim Community.

'Steps to implement administrative and economic reforms continued throughout 1970 and 1971. Schools and hospitals were reopened. Vocational training centres were established in Wau, Juba and Malakal. More Southerners were appointed to top administrative, police, and diplomatic posts. Sunday was recognised as the weekly holiday in the South. A delegation from the All Africa Conference of Churches was invited to the Sudan. It visited the South and on its return, S. H. Amissah, the General Secretary of the Conference, wrote that they had been encouraged to see the efforts of the Churches to come to grips with some of the problems created by the unsettled state of affairs in the past.[12] They confirmed that the situation, compared to the past, was easier, and hoped that "the policy of the Government of regional autonomy for the South will help not only to accelerate progress but also to foster improved relationships, as the policy is vigorously implemented".[13]

The mission found out that there was a sincere desire by the Government, the Southerners they had met and the Church leaders in the Sudan for reconciliation rather than military operations. According to K. E. Ankrah, Africa Secretary of the Division of Inter-Church Aid, Refugees and World Service of the World Council of Churches,[14] the report of the mission was hotly contested in some quarters, especially among ex-missionary groups, but on the whole it was generally accepted that a path had been paved which should be followed. The mission recommended the initiation of discussions with the Government about the shaping of the expected autonomy.

A joint mission of the World Council of Churches and the All-Africa Conference of Churches visited the Sudan in April 1971. This time the World Council of Churches became convinced that the problem was not religious but had 'a

complexity of reasons – which might include religion, race,
political, social and economic factors – all of which had
combined to create a political problem'.[15] It also became
convinced that 'the Church leaders should approach the
Sudan problem from a political angle'.[16]

This change of attitude was welcomed by the Sudan
Government. When the joint delegation mentioned above
visited Khartoum in May 1971, the Government representatives did not question their motives. They asked their support
and assistance in the efforts for peace.

In the mean time, a group of British trade unionists
associated with the Movement for Colonial Freedom had
been invited in June 1970 to visit the Southern Sudan and
attend a Youth Festival held in Juba. The delegation
consisted of Barbara Haq (Secretary of the M.C.F.), Jack
Stern (Executive Member, National Union of Railwaymen),
Terry Trench (Executive Member, Association of Cine
Technicians), Harry Kayl (London Organizer and Executive
Member, National Union of Tailoring and Garment Workers)
and Joe Holmes (President of the Kent Mineworkers). This
followed a visit by a delegation of British Members of
Parliament in October 1970, consisting of Robert Edwards,
Joan Lestor, John Preston, David Clark, and Roy Carter.

The visits of these two delegations were part of the efforts
of the Government to obtain support in the outside world for
its new policy. There was special concern at the hostile
publicity that the new policy was receiving in Britain as a
result of the activities of the Southern Sudan Association in
London. The Chairman of the Association's Board of
Management was B. H. D. MacDermot and its Director was
Mading deGarang. The former recruited to his association a
number of personalities in Britain known for their opposition
to reconciliation and the unity of the Sudan. The Southern
Sudan Association and its publication *The Grass Curtain* was
in fact no more than an arm of the Anya Nya in Britain.

The Army began to take a positive interest in the areas of
construction by contributing towards the reconstruction of
roads and the setting up of co-operative societies. Organisations of Youth, Women and Trade Unionists were being
created as part of the developing socialist democratic

movement. In January 1971 a conference on economic and social development in the South was held in Juba, organised by the School of Extra-Mural Studies in the University of Khartoum and attended by leading ministers and civil servants. Two British economists were invited at the suggestion of the Movement for Colonial Freedom.

The conference was successful in bringing together Northern and Southern Sudanese intellectuals, in focusing on the problems of economic and social development, and in making recommendations on the priorities. An issue which attracted much discussion was the cultural and language aspect. The Southern intellectuals emphasized the need for the promotion of their own culture and languages, arguing that this was not only the correct 'socialist path' to be followed by a socialist government but a necessary step in the promotion of unity in the South.

Delegations of Southern personalities were sent to neighbouring countries to explain the new policy to the refugees and leaders outside the country. The Minister for Southern Affairs visited Uganda, where he conferred with Pope Paul VI during the latter's visit, and later London and New York. Abel Alier visited East Africa, and in March 1971 led a delegation of Northerners and Southerners to the Scandinavian countries and held meetings with the Committee for Voluntary Organisations in Geneva, the World Council of Churches and with the Pope in Rome. The Pope expressed his wish to help in the efforts for reconciliation. The sincere efforts of the Government were recognised and the Vatican promised its official support for the new policy.

These activities were supplemented by efforts at the level of relations with neighbouring countries and regional organisations. General Nimeiri visited the Central African Republic, Chad, Zaire and Ethiopia, and Heads of States from these countries were invited to the Sudan. Trade agreements were signed with Ethiopia, Chad, Zaire and Uganda. The agreement with Uganda signed in August 1970 embraced trade and economic co-operation: President Obote endorsed the new policy, and the Uganda Government set out to encourage politicians and refugees to return to the Sudan.

The agreement signed in March 1971 by the Sudanese and

Ethiopian Ministers of Foreign Affairs was perhaps the most important agreement in the direction of solving the Southern problem: the two Governments agreed[17] to

1. Take all necessary measures in order to put an end to all forms of subversive activities directed against the other including such activities as may take place across their common borders.
2. Prohibit the activities of all subversive organisations.
3. Disarm all rebel elements and dismantle their camps.
4. Expel all rebel and dissident leaders as may be identified by the Government concerned and take such measures as may be necessary to prevent the return of such leaders.
5. Adhere to all international, regional and bilateral conventions, and the decisions, resolutions and declarations of the O.A.U. governing the status of refugees.
6. Take all necessary measures to encourage the voluntary repatriation of refugees and accord all facilities to official representatives to visit refugee camps.
7. Remove refugee camps to a distance of at least fifty miles from the common borders.
8. Restrict the activities of missionary organisations to humanitarian work.
9. Organize and supervise the peaceful settlement and subsistence of refugees in their camps.

It was also agreed to form two joint commissions to inspect suspected rebel camps on both sides of the border. The agreement paved the way for a new attitude of co-operation between the two countries. The old suspicions began to give way to a realization that positive co-operation would help to solve their respective problems. This attitude was confirmed in November 1971 when President Nimeiri visited Ethiopia. The final[18] communiqué on the visit stated:

The two Heads of State reaffirmed their determination to remove all obstacles which are likely to hamper good neighbourly relations. They have agreed that relations between the countries continue to be guided by strict observance of the principles of non-interference and respect for territorial integrity and that all agreements between the Sudan and Ethiopia should be implemented with deliberate speed. They have in particular agreed to take all necessary measures not to allow their respective territories to be used for acts directed against the national unity and territorial integrity of the other.

In addition to this, President Nimeiri continued to attend the O.A.U. meetings of Heads of States and explain the new policy on the Southern Sudan. The leaders of the liberation movements in Africa were invited to establish offices in Khartoum. The Sudan paid its contributions to the O.A.U. Liberation Committee funds. The object of this was to emphasize the Sudan's commitment to African policies and project an image of a country committed to a radical and progressive policy.

These steps no doubt had their positive results in the improvement of conditions in the South. A growing number of refugees was returning. More Southern students were returning to the Sudan: a group of those resident in Uganda visited the country in September 1969 and went back better informed, and persuaded of the Government's seriousness and the improvement of conditions. In January 1970, all ministries and government departments were directed that any ex-employees who decided to return to the country should be re-employed immediately and no disciplinary action taken against them. They were re-employed in the same jobs and at the same levels as when they departed.

There was more participation in decision-making and in political activities by Southerners in both the South and the North, but this did not convince the Southern political leaders abroad nor the Anya Nya. The latter continued in their previous policy. The confrontation between the Sudanese Army and the Anya Nya continued as before with the only difference that each party was better equipped. There was criticism too from some Southerners inside the Sudan. Natale Olwak, a Southern lecturer in law at the University of Khartoum, wrote in January 1971:[19]

It is now two years since the government declared its policy towards the South and no one knows yet the form the autonomy promised to the South will take. It is true that it was stated in the policy statement that the building of a broad socialist-oriented democratic movement in the South, forming part of the revolutionary structure in the

North and capable of assuming the rights of power in that region and rebuffing imperialist penetration and infiltration from the rear, is an essential pre-requisite for the practical and healthy application of regional autonomy. But this pre-requisite is not in any way contradicted by defining the powers that are to be exercised by the Autonomous South within a united Sudan. Transfer of government leadership to democratically-elected bodies in the South will have to await the creation of such bodies in the whole of the Democratic Republic of the Sudan.

Though the Declaration of June calls for a period of preparation for the time when regional organs of state power will come into being, there is definitely a need to move faster to achieve results which will win the confidence of the people.

Serious questions have to be answered as soon as possible: When will it be possible to establish the political organs of regional power? What form are they to take? What are to be the powers of the region? Until we have answered the above questions no real effective political action can be taken in realization of regional autonomy. It is not possible to establish a Ministry of Southern Affairs with full executive responsibility before what constitutes 'Southern Affairs' is defined. I see the need for popular discussion of the powers that shall be granted to the Autonomous South. Since the 9 June Declaration is committed to the regional autonomy in which power is exercised by democratic institutions, the Government can now define the powers and let these powers be exercised by the Minister of Southern Affairs until such powers are transferred to regional organs.

In the view of many Southerners at the time, the 'socialist democratic movement could not have been built overnight, and since the urgent problem for the Southerners at that time was how soon the Government was to implement its policy, to make them wait until such time as the movement was to have been built was to set a stage for suspicion and mistrust among the Southerners'.[20] The Ministry of Southern Affairs was seen as being at fault for its emphasis on economic development of the South as a means of solving the political problem, and by so doing choosing to 'ignore the fact that the South was caught up in a political economic vicious circle'.[21]

In a memorandum sent to the President and Members of the Revolutionary Council in November 1970, the Southern Youth and Students Organisations in Khartoum showed concern with the pace of the implementation of the new policy:[2 2]

> The process of the solution is almost static, the details of the regional self-rule are not yet out, which makes us feel that the Declaration of regional self-rule will be but ink on paper. In fact, apart from a few steps taken in promotion and appointment of Southerners, the political programme of the Government towards the South is largely unclear. The share of the South in the Five-Year Development Plan is less than one-eighth of the whole budget, a step which is even more discouraging. The Ministry of State for Southern Affairs, which was supposed to hurry up with the implementation of the solution, is still a ministry without powers.

These criticisms and expressions of dissatisfaction with the Government's approach in the implementation of regional autonomy from groups supporting the new policy were most obvious among a newly-formed political association of Southerners in Khartoum – the Southern Sudan Intellectuals Association. Its membership was made up of educated Southerners in Khartoum, the majority of whom had belonged in the past to either S.A.N.U. or the Southern Front. This group continued to criticise the slowness in implementing the new policy.

Another area of discontent and disillusionment related to the Government's policy of alignment with the Arab world. The Government had increasingly shown this during 1969 and 1970, especially in its relations with Egypt and Libya. Southern intellectuals and the leaders outside the country viewed this link at the time as a negation of its policy of closer links with its African neighbours, and as a contradiction of the principles contained in the 9 June Declaration. The Tripoli Agreement signed by the Sudan, Libya and Egypt was further viewed with great apprehension by the Southerners, as a step towards a larger union with the Sudan's neighbours in the Arab world. A statement by Nimeiri in Cairo in November 1970 that 'the three countries, Libya,

Egypt and the Sudan, could possibly struggle in Africa to defend the Arab civilization which is being encircled and hampered by imperialism in an attempt to stop its influx in the heart of Africa',[23] produced the strongly worded memorandum by Southern students and youth organisations in Khartoum already referred to. The aims of the union of the three states and the statement of the President in Cairo that the Southern people had no culture of their own was, according to the memorandum, 'alarming, and it greatly contradicts the terms of the declared policy towards the South'.[24]

The memorandum went on as follows:

> It has been our belief that the Sudan, as an Afro-Arab country, has a leading role to play in both the African and the Arab world. The principle on which the Sudan has joined the union with Egypt and Libya has nullified its effective role in Afro-Arab relations. This move is to be regretted in view of the fact that the Sudan, having common borders with six African states, should have been expected to step up her relations with them more than it has done with the Arab states. We feel that the African world, where the Sudan could play a greater role, has been completely neglected. In this respect we say that the Sudan is basically an Afro-Arab state, and this should be admitted not in words or slogans but in practice, and any trends in foreign policy should always take into account the ethnic composition of the country.[25]

A third area of discontent referred to in the memorandum was the Government's educational policy which, it was argued, contradicted the June declaration of regional autonomy. The new educational policy had unified the educational system in the country, thus abolishing the village schools and using Arabic as the only medium of instruction up to secondary school level. This was seen as a replacement of African by Arab cultural values, thus contradicting the spirit of the June Declaration. There was heated discussion of this issue at the Erkawit Conference held in Juba in January 1971. The educated Southerners seemed to have reached a position very different from the official policy explained by the Minister of Education. On the other hand, the Southern political leaders outside the Sudan continued their opposition to the new policy both internationally and nationally. At the international level they sent a note signed by Lawrence Wol Wol and F. B. Maggot, representing the Southern Sudan Liberation Front, to the President of the United Nations General Assembly and the U.N. Secretary-General. The note reiterated the old accusations against the North – domination of the South by Arabs, the denial to the Africans of the South of participation in the Government, religious persecution, social discrimination and domination, genocide, the spread of famine and disease and the absence of education or health facilities.[26] The note accused the Arab nations such as Egypt, Libya, Algeria and Kuwait, together with the Soviet Union and East Germany, of providing both financial and military support to the Northern Sudanese[27] to conduct the military operations against the African South. In their note they asked the United Nations 'to appoint an international committee to investigate the desperate situation of the people in the Southern Sudan and of the refugees in the neighbouring African states, to urge the International Red Cross to send food and medicines, to urge member-states of the United Nations to voice their indignation over the policy of genocide by the Sudanese Arabs against the Africans of Southern Sudan . . . to persuade the U.A.R., Soviet Union and eleven other countries involved to stop the supply of arms and armaments to the Sudan'.[28]

A month later, in December 1970, a letter from the same signatories to the President of the U.N. General Assembly referred to genocide and suffering in the Southern Sudan and appealed for intervention by the U.N. As a result of these activities, representations were also made to the U.N. Commission on Human Rights in Geneva. The U.N. Association of New York issued in December 1970 a resolution on the Southern Sudan in which it called upon the U.N. to undertake a formal investigation of the situation in the South and suggested the establishment of a peace-keeping force to restore the rights of the Southerners. The Anti-Slavery Society presented a statement to the Commission's Chairman in March 1971 on what it called the violation of human rights taking place in the Sudan, and appealed for action by the U.N.

It was evident from this note and other activities that after May 1969 the Southern political leaders were becoming increasingly hostile to the Arab world generally and to Egypt in particular. At the same time in their meetings and communications they expressed increasing hostility towards the Soviet Union with which the Government had close and friendly relations at the time. *Grass Curtain*, which replaced *Voice of the Southern Sudan* as their organ of publicity and was published in London by the Southern Sudan Association, reflected these hostile attitudes, and committees for the support of the Anya Nya and its political associations were established in Rome and in Norway. Southern political leaders now stepped up their activities in Europe and Africa.

The Norwegian Association for the Southern Sudan was particularly active. The Norwegian section of the Association for the Study of the World Refugee Problem adopted a resolution condemning repression and persecution in the South and urging that help be given to the rebels. The Bishop of Oslo in February 1971 addressed a letter on the Southern Sudan to the U.N. Commission on Human Rights urging it to investigate the situation. A fund-raising campaign in support of the refugees was conducted in the Scandinavian countries in April 1971.

The purpose of these committees was to obtain help and assistance for the Anya Nya and act as pressure-groups on their governments and political parties and liaison between the Southern politicians and the press and other communications media. It was possible through these committees and through direct contacts to give wide publicity to the problem of the South and present the North as an oppressor and Communist-dominated.

International and national relief organisations were caught up in the campaign through the assistance they gave to the rebels. These organisations, many of which were involved in the Biafra war, redirected their efforts to the Southern Sudan. An article in *The Sunday Times* of London on 1 March 1970 compared the problem of the Southern Sudan with that of Biafra, and reported that[29] 'the same Western European Church organisations which ran Uli airstrip in Biafra supply large quantities of medical supplies, food and clothing to the 250,000 Southern Sudanese refugees in neighbouring countries'.

The motives of these organisations varied: some looked at it as a religious war against Islam, some as a war against the Arabs, some as an anti-Egyptian war and some as a fight against Communism. The organisations which were particularly active in their support included Caritas International, Caritas (West Germany), Church Relief Work (West Germany) Action Committee for Africa – Biafra and Southern Sudan (West Germany) and the Verona Fathers (Italy).

Individuals such as David Robinson, an American journalist, Storrs McCall, a lecturer in Makerere University, Uganda, Franz Gypkens of the Africa Society in Frankfurt, West Germany, Ruth Bouvert of Action Medico (headquarters in West Germany), Gunter Kaplan of Cologne, West Germany, and Eliman Fürstenberg, and others, became involved and provided help in the form of arms, medicine, publicity and finance.[30]

A privately owned airline company in Kampala – 'Southern Air-Motive' – owned by Beverley Barnard and Anthony Divall, both British, arranged the transport of arms. The Anya Nya representatives in Europe, Kampala, Nairobi, Zaire and Addis Ababa acted as liaison between these individuals and organisations on the one hand and the rebels in the South on the other hand.

There had been reports of support from other individuals, organisations and governments but the two most important sources were Israel and the mercenaries.

Israeli involvement in the Southern problem went as far back as 1963. The early reports of this involvement were mainly about contacts made by Southern political leaders with Israeli embassies in Uganda, Ethiopia, Congo and Chad. Israel's involvement in the Southern problem increased after the 1967 war in the Middle East. Arms, advisers and training facilities were particularly evident after 1969.

A study made for the World Council of Churches reported the following:

Israel began supplying arms to the resistance forces in the South in 1969. This involvement has gradually increased and is reported by a number of sources. In an article on the Sudan in *The Sunday Times* ('Biafra Tragedy threatens South Sudanese Rebels', 1 March 1970) it was reported that refugees from the Sudan area had informed religious groups in Italy and West Germany that Israel is now able to supply arms and military know-how (through small groups of technical advisers) to the Christian South Sudanese guerrillas. This increase in aid had been made possible by the military missions which Israel had established in neighbouring countries. The latter evidently refers to the Israeli mission training insurgency troops for the Ethiopian armed forces and perhaps also to the Israeli presence in Uganda at the time.[31]

As to the nature and extent of Israeli aid to the South, the study stated that

arms and supplies are flown in by an unmarked DC–3 piloted by an Israeli and dropped to Anya Nya waiting in the Bush. Weapons include heavy machine-guns, bazookas, hand grenades, .303 World War II rifles and old landmines. Many of these are of British and Russian origin and were captured by Israel during the Six Day War. Israel is further reported to have trained twenty-six Southerners in Israel and to have a small mission of advisors at Torit.[32]

Two French journalists, Claude Deffarge and Gordian Troller, who were able to visit the area controlled by the rebels at the time, wrote as follows:

International politics on a grand scale has found a foothold in the Southern Sudan. Up to September 1969 foreign intervention was confined to certain religious groups who furnished money and medicine to their followers only. At present it is conditioned by the international confrontations; Israel tries to use the black revolt as part of its own war with the Arabs.[33]

The article revealed the presence of Israeli military advisers and an Israeli lady doctor in the South, and the training of Anya Nya officers in Israel.

A year later the American journalist David Robison wrote the following:

... We drove across the Sudanese frontier at night when the border guards were sound asleep. I was startled by the well equipped appearance of Steiner's 110 soldiers. They carried British rifles and Russian bazookas and on the brims of their bush hats they wore brass Anya Nya emblems, 'Made in Israel', bragged one soldier. Then I noticed a Russian machine-gun. 'Where did you get that?' I asked Steiner. 'From the Six Day War', he replied with a grin. Steiner explained that the Israelis, fearful of being outflanked along the Red Sea by their Soviet and Arab foes, had given the Anya Nya some of the weapons they had captured from the Egyptians in 1967. Rebel officers boasted that thirty of their comrades had been sent to Israel for three months, 'and now they are second-lieutenants', he sniffed. 'In a European army, it takes three months basic training to make a private and two years to make a good second-lieutenant.'[34]

The Israeli Ambassador in Kampala was not only in touch with the leaders of the Anya Nya but he attended some of their meetings held in Kampala.[35] Israel had found it in her own interest to interfere as a diversionary tactic in her war against the Arab countries.

As for the mercenaries, the most notorious were Rolf Steiner and F. Bullingham, a Briton whose real name is Alexander Gay. Bullingham or Gay was a mercenary in both the Congo and Biafra.[36] He came to the Southern Sudan and, together with Steiner, helped to infiltrate arms to the Anya Nya.

Steiner, a West German by nationality and once a member of the Hitler Youth organisation, joined the French Army in 1947 and stayed in it for twenty years, serving in Indochina, Korea, Algeria, Madagascar and Suez. He went to Biafra in 1967 as a military adviser to Ojukwu, but left Biafra in 1968, claiming that this was because of his refusal to persuade General Ojukwu to agree to the French proposal that French oil companies should be allowed to control oil production in Biafra after the war.[37] From Biafra he went to Gabon, and then to South Africa, Rhodesia, Portugal, Switzerland and Italy.

He told of his involvement in the Southern question in a statement to the Uganda Government on his arrest in October 1970:

At that time I had not yet known about Southern Sudan's problems. I first heard about Southern Sudan when I was in Rome. I was fully briefed about the Sudan by some Verona Fathers who worked in the Sudan before. The Fathers compared the Sudan problems with Biafran problem. I entered Uganda for the first time at the end of June 1969. I met Serafino Wani Swaka, a teacher at the Lubiri secondary school. He was introduced to me by Father Agostini who is now the Superior-General of the Verona Fathers in Rome. His address was also given by the Forderungsgesellschaft Afrika (Organisation for development of Africa — excluding Arab countries). I went to Arua by a chartered plane . . . While I was at Arua an Anya Nya called Simon Shada agreed to take me to the Uganda-Sudan border. We walked on foot from Keri to the border. I spent four days before being introduced to General Taffeng. General Taffeng was aware of my arrival because of a letter which had already been sent to him. The General gave his guards to take me to different camps in the Southern Sudan. My main mission was to see conditions in the Southern Sudan and report back to Germany. The mission took about two weeks . . . When I was in Kampala I met Beverley Barnard who had arrived from Britain via Nairobi. Barnard told me that he was once a British diplomat.

I went back to Germany on 5 August 1969. I reported the result of my mission to the organisation which sent me to Southern Sudan. I remained there for 2½ months. I returned to Uganda at the end of October 1969 through Entebbe. I had seven boxes of medicine with me. The boxes were addressed to the Bishop of Kampala with a letter that he should arrange for the delivery of medicine to the Sudanese refugees. After three days I left Kampala for Southern Sudan. During my stay in the Sudan I built two airstrips — one at Mortu and another at Kenyiba which is only 8 km. (5 miles) from Kajo where Sudanese troops are based. I also built two hospitals and three dispensaries. One of the dispensaries was bombed by the Sudan Army on 25 September 1970. The airstrips have never been used for landing. They are only used for dropping supplies . . . Already 20,000,000 dollars have been raised in Germany to assist the Southerners. This is mainly for medical supplies. When I was arrested on 4 October 1970, I was on my way to Germany to inform them about the assistance and progress. I came to Uganda ostensibly as a tourist so that I should not be suspected. If Uganda refused me permission to enter through Entebbe or anywhere at once by declaring me a prohibited immigrant, I would pass through other countries such as Ethiopia, Congo or Kenya. I also knew a Father called Philip Abas who has a base on Nuba Mountain. I have no connection with his organisation. He was in Uganda in July 1970 and later met Col. Joseph Lagu, who is at Owing Kibul. He is stronger than Taffeng, whose arrest he ordered in April 1970.[38]

The information given in this statement was later confirmed by Steiner during his trial in Khartoum. He talked at length about the involvement of the Israelis and of West German voluntary organisations, and his participation in the attacks made by the Anya Nya on Sudanese Army posts.

When the Sudanese Army attacked Mortu in October 1970, Steiner fled across the border to Uganda where he was arrested and interrogated, and made the statement quoted above. In spite of pressure on Uganda from Israel, West Germany, Church organisations and supporters of the Anya Nya not to hand Steiner over to the Sudan Government, President Obote decided to do so, and Steiner was given a public trial in Khartoum in August 1971.

The Steiner trial demonstrated the extent of outside involvement in the Southern Sudan problem. In that trial Steiner voluntarily uncovered the details of the Anya Nya organisation and the financial and military assistance they received. He also uncovered the conflicts and divisions between the different groups and the leadership. The public inside and outside the Sudan came to learn for the first time about the dangerous war in the South and its dimensions. The verdict of the court was to find him guilty, and he was sentenced to twenty years' imprisonment.

The external involvement — as exemplified by Israel, the mercenaries, Church and voluntary organisations and individuals — added a new dimension to the conflict between North and South. It was already clear by the middle of 1971 that in spite of the sincerity and seriousness of the Government in its desire to implement the policy of regional autonomy, there were many difficulties in the way. Economic difficulties, opposition from the political groups which had been overthrown, and differences with the Communist Party occupied much of the Government's time and energy.

The policy of the Ministry of Southern Affairs, which was more concerned with economic development and the establishment of a democratic socialist movement than with a definition of regional autonomy and the working out of the details of the administrative and constitutional structures, was not always supported by all the Southerners in Khartoum. Furthermore, Southern politicians outside the Sudan were waiting for more positive steps in the direction of regional autonomy.

The divisions within the Government between 'Arabists' and 'Non-Arabists' and between 'Communists' and 'Non-Communists' were factors which contributed further to the delay in taking positive steps in solving the problem, and thereby added to suspicions and accusations. Southern politicians outside the Sudan did not sympathise with the Government's policy, which advocated friendship with the Soviet Union and with the Arab countries while condemning the West.

The implementation of the 9 June Declaration had received great support in the North and the South, and a number of positive and constructive steps had been taken, but these by themselves were not enough to stop the armed conflict and clear the way for peace. This is not to say that conditions in both North and South for establishing peace did not improve; in spite of the build up of arms on both sides – possibly because of this – conditions did not only improve but the chances for peace became greater than they had been before June 1969. Efforts in the economic, educational and social fields, together with the establishment of good relations with the Sudan's African neighbours, resulted in some progress and optimism.

However, a situation had developed in which it was necessary to have a new and different approach so that a breakthrough could finally be achieved.

REFERENCES

1. Appendix I.

2. Abel Alier, quoted in D. M. Wai, *op. cit.*, p. 27.

3. Ministry of Southern Affairs, *A Revolution in Action*, No. 2: speeches by Joseph U. Garang, Khartoum (undated).

4. Natale Olwak, 'Regional Autonomy for the South', paper in the Fifth Erkawit Conference, Juba, January 1971, mimeographed, p. 30.

5. Quoted in N. Olwak, *op. cit.*, p. 8. Also Report on the work of the Constitution Amendment Commission by the Chairman, Justice R. C. Stanley-Baker, Khartoum, 1951.

6. *Ibid.*

7. *Ibid.*

8. *Ibid.*

9. Information from the Refugees' Office, Ministry of Interior, Khartoum.

10. N. Olwak, *op. cit.*, p. 34.

11. Ministry of Southern Affairs, *A Revolution in Action*, No. 3. Speech by Abel Alier delivered at Makerere University, Uganda, 9 February, 1970.

12. Letter from S. H. Amissah, General Secretary, All Africa Council of Churches, to Minister for Southern Affairs, Nairobi, 2 July 1970.

13. *Ibid.*

14. E. Ankrah, 'Sudan, The Church and Peace' in *Africa*, No. 9, May 1972, pp. 58–63.

15. *Ibid.*

16. *Ibid.*

17. Agreement between the Imperial Ethiopian Government and the Government of the Democratic Republic of the Sudan, 24 March 1971, Khartoum.

18. Joint Communiqué between Sudan and Ethiopia, Khartoum, 7 November 1971.

19. N. Olwak, *op. cit.*, pp. 34–5.

20. Ministry of Foreign Affairs, *Peace and Unity in the Sudan*, Khartoum 1973, p. 43.

21. *Ibid.*

22. Memorandum to the President and Members of the Revolutionary Command Council by Southern students – Youth Organisation, Khartoum, 19 November 1970.

23. *Al Ahram* newspaper, Cairo, 8 November 1970.

24. Memorandum to the President, *op. cit.*

25. *Ibid.*

26. Letter addressed to the President, U.N. General Assembly, New York, November 1970, and letter addressed to the Secretary-General, U.N., New York, November 1970.

27. *Ibid.*

28. *Ibid.*

29. *Sunday Times*, 1 March 1970.

30. Information from the Steiner trial Khartoum August 1971.

31. Theresa Scherf, 'The Sudan Conflict', study prepared for the World Council of Churches, Geneva, 1971, mimeographed.

32. *Ibid.*

33. *Le Nouvel Observateur*, 17–23 August 1970.

34. David Robinson, *Newsweek,* 10 May 1971.

35. Information from the Steiner trial, *op. cit.*

36. M. O. Beshir, *The Mercenaries and Africa*, Khartoum 1972.

37. Information from the Steiner trial, *op. cit.*

38. *Ibid.*

CHAPTER V

STEPS LEADING TO THE ADDIS ABABA AGREEMENT

The opportunity for the breakthrough came in July 1971. Abel Alier, who had always taken an active part in the attempts to reach a solution, became Minister of Southern Affairs after the abortive Communist coup of July 1971. The Communists, who were being blamed for the delay in the implementation of the policy for regional autonomy, and being accused of using their official positions to further their partisan interests and obstructing the Government's policies towards the South, were removed from office and from positions of influence.[1]

Abel Alier's appointment was widely supported by the educated Southerners inside and outside the Sudan. His first action on assuming office as Minister of Southern Affairs was to obtain the new Government's agreement to start negotiations with the Southern political leaders inside and outside the Sudan with a view to implementing regional autonomy as soon as practical.

It would be wrong to conclude that no attempts for negotiations with the exiles had ever taken place in the previous two years. The visits undertaken to Europe and East Africa by different delegations and individuals already referred to were part of the attempts to prepare the ground for such negotiations. Contacts with Southern leaders outside the Sudan were being conducted through the World Council of Churches. The World Council and the All Africa Conference of Churches mission which visited the Sudan in May 1971, once it had become convinced that the Sudan Government was serious in its desire for peace and reconciliation, set out to make contacts with these leaders. Immedi-

ately after returning to Europe, the mission began to make
contacts with the Southern leaders in both Africa and
Europe. The following letter was sent on 6 August 1971 from
the office of the Commission of the Churches on International Affairs to the Southern representatives in Europe:

> We are pleased that following several conversations with
> you as the delegated representatives of the Anya Nya in
> Europe, during which you informed us of the present
> position of your movement; and following the visit of a
> joint World Council of Churches/All Africa Conference of
> Churches mission to Khartoum, where we were given the
> Sudan Government's position on reconciliation and relief,
> we are now able to help make your journey to Africa
> possible. This we do out of our sincere interest that a
> peace be established in the Sudan which will make possible
> a creative use of the relief assistance to the suffering
> Sudanese which the Churches stand ready to give as soon
> as it can be determined that such assistance can be
> properly supervised and distributed.
>
> You have been fully informed about our visit to
> Khartoum, where we were asked to enter into conversa-
> tions with you which might lead to negotiations between
> the two parties in the conflict. It is our understanding that,
> despite the events which have occurred in the interim,
> these positions remain firm and can be considered those of
> the Khartoum Government. We have a standing invitation
> to return to Khartoum for further discussions in which we
> would hopefully be able to faithfully represent the views
> of the Southern Sudanese leadership. We therefore look
> forward to having a report of your visit on your return. We
> hope that it will (a) include the reaction of your leadership
> to the positions stated by the Khartoum Government;
> (b) obtain a list of Southerners whom Anya Nya leaders
> would want to be involved with in negotiations; and
> (c) obtain letters of credence stating who in fact Col. Lagu
> wishes to authorise to deal with the W.C.C./A.A.C.C. on
> behalf of the Anya Nya.
>
> Allow me to repeat that the W.C.C. has offered its
> services to you and to the Khartoum Government as a
> politically disinterested international humanitarian organ-
> isation. Our sole motive is to best serve the people of
> Sudan, North and South, for whom we understand that a
> lasting peace is indispensable.

Please convey our greetings to Col. Lagu and the other leaders of the Southern Sudan.[2]

In August 1971, Mading deGarang and Lawrence Wol Wol reported after a visit to Africa that the Southern leadership was prepared to enter into negotiations with a view to finding a peaceful settlement to the conflict within the framework of one Sudan.[3]

Of equal importance and more significance were the contacts and negotiations going on in London through the Movement for Colonial Freedom. The involvement of the M.C.F. in the Southern Sudan question had begun in January 1970, when a resolution was proposed by organisations affiliated to the M.C.F. condemning the treatment of the people of the South by the Sudan Government. The annual national delegate conference which met on 14/15 March 1970, which Mading deGarang and Jacob Akol – both of the Southern Sudan Association in London and of the *Grass Curtain* publication – and Ali Abu Sin of the Sudan Embassy in London were invited to attend, rejected the proposed resolution. Instead, the Conference resolved that the M.C.F. should endeavour to use its good offices to bring about some kind of rapprochement between exiled Southerners and the Sudan Government.[4] Barbara Haq, as Secretary of the M.C.F., pursued the question with the Sudan Ambassador in London and the Minister of State for Southern Affairs during the latter's visit to London in April 1970. As a result of these discussions, the visits by the group of British trade unionists and by the British Members of Parliament already referred to were arranged as ways of informing British public opinion on the issues involved. A meeting was arranged by Barbara Haq between the Ambassador and Mading deGarang on 2 August 1970: both became convinced that there was a basis for preliminary negotiations based on proposals put forward by Mading deGarang on behalf of the Anya Nya. This was communicated to the Sudan Government of Khartoum. Writing to Joseph Garang in Khartoum on 10 August 1970 Barbara Haq said:

> I have held a number of discussions with Mading de-Garang, editor of the *Grass Curtain*, and through him with Lawrence Wol Wol who is in Paris. I found that there was a

genuine respect for the present Government of Sudan, that many of their proposed measures were favourably viewed, and that provided there is an expansion of the statements already made on Autonomy for the South, there would be every possibility of its acceptance by the Anya Nya. I am informed that all the exiled provisional governments have now been dissolved and that the sole political leadership of the exiled Southerners rests in the Anya Nya led by Lagu.

The view held by Mading and Lawrence is that the return of individual political leaders to Sudan would not help in the long run, and that only a political settlement which ends the fighting will enable real development of the South to take place. They, therefore, requested me to put forward the following proposals:

1. That there should be a private statement from your Government outlining in more detail what is intended by Autonomy for the South, and that at the same time a schedule should be given for the fulfilment of the proposals provided that there is a ceasefire and full co-operation from the Anya Nya.

2. That these proposals should be privately conveyed through me, as General Secretary of the M.C.F., to Lawrence and Mading, who would in turn visit East Africa and consult with the Anya Nya leaders. Any points to be clarified would then be conveyed back to you and your Government for further consideration.

3. When there appears to be a basis for agreement, Tanzania, Uganda or Zambia should be asked to act as host to a meeting between you and your Government and the Anya Nya leaders for talks on a ceasefire and agreement on plans for Autonomy.

It is essential that the first two steps should be completely private and not publicized and take place indirectly through me. Mading has made it quite clear to me that they are aware of the motivation of their supporters here and that because of the clean record of our Movement they feel they can act through us in this matter.

Proposals of the nature suggested may not be accepted by all the leaders of the Anya Nya. But if a clean offer on the nature of Autonomy is given to them, there is every chance that a major part would accept and that remnants there carrying on fighting would become isolated . . .

It would also enable many of the former politicians now

in exile to return to assist in building the South in a way which the present offer of amnesty does not afford. . . .[5]

These proposals were further discussed in a meeting held in London in September 1970 between Joseph Garang and Mading deGarang and other Southerners. It was agreed that six Southerners of their choice should come to London to meet Mading and others supporting the Anya Nya, who in turn would communicate with the leaders and with Joseph Lagu. The meeting was held in Barbara Haq's flat and the only outsider attending was B. H. D. MacDermot, Chairman of the Southern Sudan Association; it was felt, according to some of those who attended the meeting, that his contributions to that meeting were not helpful.

The six Southerners proposed by Mading for the discussions were: Franco Garang, Samuel Aru, Cleto Hassan, Hilary Logali, Natale Olwak and Canon Amosa. Both Uganda and London were suggested as possible places for the meeting. In either case some of the Anya Nya leaders would attend.[6]

I myself came to London in October 1970 on my way to New York for the U.N. General Assembly. At the suggestion of Mading deGarang, made through Barbara Haq, we met together with Jacob Akol in the offices of the *Grass Curtain*. Our discussions covered the same ground. We agreed that negotiations could only be held if the principle of the unity of the Sudan were accepted and separation excluded. We also agreed that negotiations between the representatives of the Sudan Government and the Anya Nya should be carried out in secret, and nothing should be made public before the outline of an agreement had been reached. We both agreed that methodology was more important than other considerations since by adopting the right method and approach to the negotiations, positive results could be achieved. I knew from Mading deGarang that this would not be an easy thing as far as the Anya Nya, or at least part of its leadership, was concerned. After three hours' talk and in spite of all the difficulties we could think of, we were both convinced that an agreement could be reached. MacDermot was not present. We both felt that the fewer outsiders brought in, the better.

At the end of October 1970 the Anya Nya leaders

accepted the principles laid down for the negotiations and the manner of the talks. Joseph Lagu, who was then the advertised leader of the South, accepted the basic principles agreed upon: one Sudan, Autonomy for the South and the necessity for a peaceful solution rather than continuation of the fighting.[7]

At the end of January 1971, however, Mading deGarang came out on behalf of the Anya Nya leadership with conditions for the negotiations to start. These conditions were:

1. cessation of all hostilities, the latter including the establishment of new posts, construction of bridges and any preparations likely to be termed military;

2. agreement for an African or O.A.U. observer team appointed from agreed African countries to be stationed in Juba, and be free to move to places like Malakal and Wau to supervise the standstill;

3. The release of Clement Mboro and all other Southern Sudanese convicted of political crimes;

4. The recognition of the Anya Nya by the Sudan Government as the only body to negotiate with — this to be publicly announced over Radio Omdurman and published in the *Sudan Gazette* and daily papers;

5. the negotiations to be held under an agreed African or O.A.U. chairmanship;

6. the talks to take place outside the Sudan.

The conditions were seen in Khartoum as a complete negation of what had been agreed upon previously. Some ministers argued that there was no point in continuing with the discussions, but others argued that the door should be left open.

This was the position which had been reached in the negotiations when the Rev. Burgess Carr of the All Africa Council of Churches contacted the Sudan Ambassador in Ethiopia in January 1971 and offered his organisation's services to assist. Efforts were mounted from different quarters and in different ways to create conditions and to reach a peace agreement. The World Council of Churches and the M.C.F. were the prime movers in this direction. In addition to this external activity, efforts were being made inside the country to promote the negotiations.

A document on the implementation of regional autonomy had already been drawn up by Abel Alier and other Southerners in Khartoum and circulated in February to various Southern Sudanese groups outside the Sudan including the Anya Nya.[8] Thus when Abel Alier assumed office in August 1971, the ground had been prepared inside and outside the Sudan for the next step in search for peace. Contacts between Southern Sudanese inside the country and those outside were resumed and stepped up. The Minister of Southern Affairs formed a committee consisting of Samuel Aru, Natale Olwak, Samuel Lubi, Musa Shol, Hilary Logali, Andrew Wieu, Cleto Hassan and Buth Diu to study and make recommendations on the main features of the permanent construction of the Democratic Republic of the Sudan and the powers of the autonomous South. The recommendations of the committee were discussed by the preparatory committee of the Sudanese Socialist Union. On the basis of these discussions, a draft act on regional self-government for the Southern Sudan was agreed upon. This draft act was circulated to Southerners inside and outside the Sudan.

Now that the first positive step was taken to clarify the 9 June Declaration by working out a detailed law defining the constitutional and administrative relations governing regional autonomy within a united Sudan, and thereby answering the criticisms of those who argued that they did not have confidence in the seriousness of the Government's policy, the way ahead towards negotiations was clear.

The second hurdle to be overcome was how, where and with whom the negotiations should be carried on. There were those inside and outside the Government who held the view that no negotiations should be carried out with rebels and that no meetings be held outside the country. They argued that this would compromise the sovereignty of the State and internationalize the problem. Others considered that the rebels were under the influence of outside forces hostile to the Government and its policies.

The solution was found in secret and unpublicized contacts. Abel Alier and Mohamed Al Baghir Ahmed, then Minister of the Interior, flew to Addis Ababa and informally met representatives of the Southern politicians living outside the Sudan. The proposed act on regional self-government was handed over to them. Agreement was reached on a tentative date and place for further negotiations.

It became clear in December 1971 that some groups among the Southern politicians and the Anya Nya opposed the peace initiative and were refusing to come forward. These groups did not then believe in the sincerity of the Government's intention to implement its policy of regional autonomy; the traditional outlook which governed the North-South relations still persisted. Some missionaries who had been involved on the side of the rebels were hostile and discouraging. Time was needed to persuade the leaders of these groups that the majority of leaders on both sides were serious in their quest for peace.

While this was going on, preparations were being made to organise a conference in Khartoum on the refugee problems. Many refugees had already responded to the peace initiatives and returned to the South. It was estimated that between June 1969 and December 1971 about 49,500 persons had returned from the neighbouring countries and an additional 80,000 had returned from the bush.[9] As more and more refugees were expected to return and it was seen that the Sudan's meagre resources would not be able to cope with the colossal problem of meeting the immediate and long-term needs of the refugees, international assistance was necessary to help solve the problem; however, this assistance was not forthcoming, because of either ignorance of the vast scope of the problem, or of what kinds of assistance were required; also, the new policy was not yet well enough known. It was thought that a meeting of potential donors was necessary to clarify the situation and persuade the international community to come forward with help and support.

A conference on relief and resettlement was held in Khartoum between 21 and 23 February 1972, attended by U.N. specialized agencies, the O.A.U. and voluntary organisations as well as observers from African and Arab countries. Representatives of some of the organisations which had assisted the rebels, such as the German Caritas and Action Medico, and journalists from European, African and Arab countries also attended.

Emergency relief projects to meet the urgent needs of the refugees and medium-term economic development projects covering agriculture, education, health, roads, communications, etc., were presented. The conference declared its support for the efforts undertaken by the Government and the willingness of the organisations attending to assist.

In the meantime, preparations for the conference in Addis Ababa between representatives of the Government and the Sudan Liberation Movement were completed. The conference was attended for the Sudan Government side by Abel Alier, Vice-President and Minister of State for Southern Affairs; Dr. Mansour Khalid, Minister for Foreign Affairs; Dr. Gaafar Mohamed Ali Bakheit, Minister for Local Government; Major-General Mohamed Al Baghir Ahmed, Minister of the Interior; and Abdel Rahman Abdalla, Minister of Public Service and Administrative Reform, Brigadier Mirghani Suleiman, and Colonel Kamal Abashar. On the side of the Southern Sudan Liberation Movement it was attended by Ezboni Mondiri, Dr. Lawrence Wol Wol, Mading deGarang, Colonel Frederick Brian Maggot, Oliver Batali Albino, Angelo Voga Morjan, the Rev. Paul Puot, and Job Adier de Jok.

Observers present included Nabiyelul Kifle, representing Emperor Haile Selassie; Leopoldo J. Niilus and Kodwo E. Ankrah, both representing the World Council of Churches; Burgess Carr, representing the All African Conference of Churches; and Samuel Athi Bwogo, representing the Sudan Council of Churches. It was agreed that Burgess Carr should act as moderator for the meetings. On 27 February 1972, the two delegations concluded and signed what came to be known as the Addis Ababa Agreement.

Immediately after, a joint meeting between the Political Bureau of the Sudanese Socialist Union – the only political party in the Sudan – and the Council of Ministers was held to discuss the Agreement. President Nimeiri held a meeting with the Army's chiefs of staff and they were briefed about the details of the Agreement. This was followed by a longer meeting attended by the Chief Justice, the magistrates, the deputy ministers, the under-secretaries and the top officers in the police and prison services for the same purpose.

On 3 March 1972, the Addis Ababa Agreement was formulated into the Regional Self-Government Act for the Southern Sudan and signed by the President. The same day, the Act was announced to the public by President Nimeiri at a mass rally in Omdurman, at which he announced that although 12 March 1972 was agreed upon as the date for a cease-fire, the army in the South had been instructed to end hostilities immediately. The date of the Agreement, 3 March, was declared Unity Day as well as a national holiday.

Regional and international response to the Agreement was favourable from the day it was signed. It was hailed from the beginning as the most important event in the recent political history of the Sudan. The London *Observer* of 27 March called it 'one of those infrequent flashes of sanity which illuminate international relations'. The *Christian Science Monitor* of 7 March wrote that the Agreement 'is an outstanding bright spot in a Middle East otherwise simmering with conspiracy and crises'. The *New York Times* of 30 March wrote: 'If successful, Sudan's new experiment in unity with diversity might even offer a useful guide to many other underdeveloped nations similarly afflicted with racial, religious and other domestic divisions.'

The African and Arab press were no less enthusiastic. The Syrian Newspaper *Al Thawra* wrote on 7 March that 'on the level of the Organisation of African Unity, the Agreement will leave a marked impression.' The *Sunday Nation* of Kenya wrote on 5 March that the 'Agreement will perhaps become one of the biggest achievements by Africa.' The Nigerian *Morning Post* of 13 March described the solution as 'one of the greatest things that has happened to the Sudan and Africa in recent months'. The Ugandan *Voice of the People* of 28 March congratulated the Sudan on its achievement and said that it was possible for the country to 'forge ahead with a bright future.' The Somali newspaper *Dawn* of 2 March hailed the accord as a proof that 'Africa's problems can and must be solved in Africa.'

Approval and support for the Agreement also came from African leaders and statesmen. In Addis Ababa the Secretary-General of the O.A.U. described the Agreement 'not only as a resounding victory for the Sudan, its people, Government and President but also, and above all, as the beginning of a new era in the peaceful settlement of African conflicts. 'This Agreement,' he went on, 'is first and foremost glaring proof of the maturity and generosity of the Africans and their ability to settle by themselves any disputes which might make them temporary

adversaries and impede their smooth and normal development.'
Amilcar Cabral, the Secretary-General of PAIGE, described the
solution as a victory in the liberation of Africa. The Heads of
States meeting in Rabat in June 1972 expressed their rejoicing
at the solution of the problem, and sent a message of support to
the President, Government and people of the Sudan.

Emperor Haile Selassie, in his speech on 28 February in
Addis Ababa to the Sudanese representatives meeting to sign
the Agreement, described it as 'of more than momentary
importance . . . It augurs well for all the people of Africa at
large.' Presidents François Tombalbaye of Chad, Bokassa of the
Central African Republic, Amin of Uganda, Siyad Barre
of Somalia, Mobutu of Zaire and Kaunda of Zambia
expressed similar feelings and support. In Cairo the Egyptian
Government released a statement which praised the Agreement and said that it opened a new era in the history of the
Sudan. The Tanzania Ministry of Foreign Affairs issued a
statement hailing it as 'a great victory for unity'; it also said
that 'the enemies of Africa and especially those who used to
exploit the problem of the Sudanese for their own reactionary ends have suffered defeat.'

The U.N. General Assembly in its twenty-seventh session
passed a resolution in which it expressed appreciation of the
efforts of the Government of the Sudan in the peaceful
settlement of the Southern Problem.

The Addis Ababa Agreement[10] and the Laws which derive
from it* defined and clarified for the first time the

*On 3 April, the following six Presidential Orders supplementing the
Regional Self-Government Act 1972 were promulgated:
1. No. 39. The Revenue of Taxes and Duties (Financial Aid and other
Revenues) for the Southern region of the Sudan.
2. No. 40. Provisional measures preceding the election of the People's
Regional Assembly.
3. No. 41. To end military operations in the Southern Region and to
establish a joint ceasefire commission.
4. No. 43. Establishment of a Special Fund to meet the expenses of
repatriation, resettlement, relief and rehabilitation of Sudanese refugees
of the Southern region.
5. No. 44. To constitute a commission and a technical committee for
the relief and rehabilitation of Sudanese refugees and expatriates of the
Southern region.
6. No. 45. To constitute a commission for the repatriation of the
Southern Sudanese refugees now residing in the neighbouring countries.

constitutional and administrative set-up which the Juba Conference, the Round Table Conference, the Twelve-Man Committee, the Political Parties Conference and the 9 June Declaration had attempted to achieve. The work of these conferences and committees had thus not been in vain.

The Agreement had a number of outstanding features. First, under the Agreement and the Act, the provinces of Bahr el Ghazal, Equatoria and Upper Nile constituted a self-governing unit within the Republic. In this way the unity of the country had been confirmed, thus meeting the wishes of the Northerners. At the same time, the wishes of the Southerners were met by having their own legislature and executive agencies. This was not a compromise but a realistic and practical formula which removed the two extreme positions, separation and the *status quo*. The national aspirations of both parties were satisfied. While the South had become a separate region, the North had not. The three provinces became part of a whole Sudan. In this way the concept of federalism, which had been looked upon in the North as a step towards separation, was removed.

Secondly, the machinery for appointing the High Executive Council in the South and the Head of the Council, which had previously been one of the areas of disagreement, was settled in a way which ensured the participation of both the regional assembly and the central national Government (as represented by the President of the Republic) in the process. The President of the High Executive Council was to represent the President and act on his behalf. The members of the High Executive Council, through being appointed by the President, became in fact representatives of the central authorities.

Thirdly, there was no separate citizenship for the Southern region, but one citizenship for the whole Sudan. The rights of all citizens were protected and guaranteed in all parts of the country. The rights of citizens to equal opportunity in education, employment, commerce and the practice of any profession were guaranteed. The fear of the Northern traders that they might not be allowed to continue their trade in the South was removed, as was discrimination against traders in commerce or taxation.

Fourthly, the question of taxation, which in earlier

discussions had been one of the areas of disagreement, had been settled in a way which would ensure control by the centre on the one hand and the right of the region to levy regional duties on the other. Taxes on economic activities originating in the South constituted the main revenue of the South. In addition, there were central Government grants. In this way a mutual financial relationship was established. Planning for economic and social development remained the responsibility of the national Government.

Fifthly, the cultural aspect of the relationship between the North and the South was maintained in the Agreement through the decision to accept Arabic as the official language of the Sudan. On the other hand, English, which is foreign to both North and South, was accepted as a principal language without prejudice to other languages. The minorities were guaranteed the freedom to use their languages and develop their own culture.

In this way the advocates of Arabic, English and the local languages were satisfied. Although educational planning became the responsibility of the national central Government, the regional assembly was given the duty of establishing and administering schools at all levels in accordance with the National Plan. By guaranteeing to parents the right to have their children educated in accordance with their own choice, the fears of Church groups were removed. The Catholics had in the past resented state interference in education.

Sixthly, the Act provided for the creation of a regional public service without specifying in detail the terms and conditions of service. It also provided for the possibility of the President making rules for the purpose of ordering relations between central and regional ministries.

The Provisional Order No. 40, published in April 1972, provided for the establishment of a Provisional High Executive Council pending the election of the People's Regional Assembly and the establishment of the High Executive Council as provided for in the Regional Self-Government Act 1972 and the Addis Ababa Agreement. The Order provided for the appointment of a President and eleven commissioners.

Abel Alier became President and the following were

appointed commissioners: Hilary Logali for Finance and
Transport; Luigi Adwok for Education; Mading deGarang for
Information, Culture and Tourism; Ezboni Mondiri for
Transport, Roads and Communications; Gamaa Hassan for
Agriculture and Animal Production; Toby Maduot for Public
Health; Elia Lupe for Regional Administration; Joseph
Oduhu for Housing and Public Utilities; Michael Taweel for
National Resources and Rural Development; and Samuel Aru
for Public Service and Labour.

The first regional government in the South therefore
included representatives of the different political groups
which were active in Southern politics inside and outside the
Sudan prior to the Agreement. The composition weighed
heavily in favour of the ex-Southern Front activists and the
ex-Anya Nya politicians and rebels. There were two S.A.N.U.
ex-politicians. Clement Mboro, the veteran Southern politician, became Chairman of the Resettlement and Rehabilitation Commission.

Although the formation of the regional government in this
way was hailed as further evidence of the growing confidence
felt by both sides, it was not satisfactory to those who had
remained inside the country. These felt that the 'outsiders'
had succeeded in obtaining most of the high posts. Others
felt that it weighed heavily in favour of the Dinka and the
Equatorians. This, however, reflected personal dissatisfaction
by small groups rather than outright opposition.

So as to emphasize the national aspect of the Agreement
and to underline the Southerners' stake in the national
government, three Southern ministers were appointed to the
central Government: Lawrence Wol Wol became the National
Minister of Planning, Bona Malwal the Minister of State for
Information and Culture and Samuel Lupai the Minister of
State for Local Government. While there were arguments that
the Southern share and participation in the central Government was less than it should be, there was criticism that the
Southerners were getting more than their full share. The
critics suggested that if it was in the national interest that
Southerners should be involved in the central national
Government, Northerners should also have been included in
the Southern regional government. This, however, would not

have been possible or practical at the time. The Southerners were concerned in the first place with the establishment of a Southern regional government which would be responsible for all aspects of life in the South.

The appointment of the Provisional High Executive Council was followed by the appointment of three commissioners to the three Southern provinces and the selection of a number of Southerners residing in the North or qualified Southerners who had remained outside the Sudan to senior administrative and technical posts. A number of senior Northern officials were therefore replaced by Southerners. By the end of June 1972, the administration of the South was fully in the hands of the Southerners.

One of the first problems faced was the clarification of relations between the region at the level of commissioners and directors and their respective counterparts in the central Government. The feeling persisted in the North that the Southern commissioners and directors were partners in a national government with special responsibilities in the South. Since this was not a federal system, they were expected to make decisions only after referring to their senior counterparts in the North. The newly-appointed senior commissioners and directors did not fully support this thesis, and it was reported that some tended to act on important matters without reference to Khartoum.

In order to overcome this problem and with a view to inspiring confidence and trust, the title 'Commissioner' was changed to 'Regional Minister'. These officials came to enjoy the same status and privileges as their colleagues and counterparts in the North. A great deal however remains to be done in this area of relations; given confidence and time, it should be possible to establish lines of communication and processes of decision-making which would promote the spirit of the Agreement and consolidate the concepts of unity in a hitherto divided country.

The other important aspect of Provisional Order No. 40 related to the election of the People's Regional Assembly within the eighteen months as provided for in the Agreement. The Order provided for the appointment of an election Commission and this was done in September 1973.

Here again, the critics were sceptical about the whole exercise. They argued that the South was in need of establishing peace, of resettling the refugees and of promoting economic development, more than anything else. Elections for a regional assembly, they argued, would distract the South from the urgent problems and cause unnecessary expense. Every minute and every pound was needed for economic development and resettlement. They were afraid that elections would revive the old rivalries and enmities among the Southerners and thus endanger the smooth implementation of the Agreement. Political conflict among the Southerners, which is natural in election campaigns, might revive dissent and dissatisfaction at a time when everything should be made to keep at least a semblance of unity and confidence.

They also argued that it was illogical to hold elections for a regional assembly, while the elections for the parent national assembly were not in view. Because of this, they argued, the elections for the regional assembly should be postponed until these issues were clarified. These arguments were rejected as being legalistic and formal. The important thing, notwithstanding the arguments against elections for the regional assembly, was to see that what was agreed upon in Addis Ababa was going to be implemented. Not to hold elections was more dangerous and would play into the hands of those who opposed the Agreement, than to hold them with all these problems recognized. These opponents continued to doubt the sincerity of the North and its desire to implement the Agreement. Those who were unhappy and dissatisfied with the formation of the Provincial High Executive Council, were only waiting for a departure from the Agreement to accuse them of a sell-out to the North and of perpetuating their recently acquired positions and privileges.

Those who advocated the holding of elections, despite all the disadvantages and risks, prevailed. The elections for the regional assembly were therefore held in November 1973. The first sitting of the assembly was in December 1973. There were sixty seats out of which thirty were territorial seats divided among Bahr el Ghazal Province (11), Equatoria Province (10) and Upper Nile (9). Thirty seats were allotted to the alliance of the Working Forces of the People.

The regional assembly elections represented the ending of one phase and the beginning of a new one. They revealed that the old political divisions and rivalries had not completely died out. Abel Alier and his group from the Ex-Southern Front and the Ex-Anya Nya politicians and sympathizers won the majority of seats. This was interpreted as a vote of confidence in those who had conducted the negotiations and as a vote of support for the Addis Ababa Agreement.

Abel Alier was nominated and elected as the first President of the High Executive Council. A new regional ministry, not very different from the first one, was formed. Thus the constitutional and administrative arrangements envisaged in the Agreement and provided for in the Provisional Order No. 40 were completed.

Outside the legal and administrative framework, the most important aspects of the Act and the protocols were those related to the resettlement of refugees and the incorporation of the Anya Nya in the national Army. The resettlement of refugees became the responsibility of the regional Government, together with the national Government – assisted by the efforts of the international organisations; for this purpose a special commission for relief and resettlement was set up and the priorities laid down. The relief and resettlement of displaced persons inside the Sudan was given priority over that of refugees coming back from outside. Although external relations were not within the powers of the regional Government, the special commission was given special powers to make contacts with external bodies and organisations in matters related to refugees and with a view to promoting its objectives.

Because of the large number of displaced persons and refugees involved and the meagre resources available in the country and from international and voluntary organisations, the aspect of the Agreement relating to refugees proved to be one of the most difficult to implement. About 190,000 Sudanese refugees were to be repatriated from Uganda, Zaire, the Central African Republic and Ethiopia, and more than 500,000 displaced persons were to be resettled. Notwithstanding this, a special fund for the South was established by presidential decree, and the special commission headed by Clement Mboro was appointed. By the end of

January 1972, 102,000 refugees had returned from abroad, and 324,000 displaced persons had returned from the countryside.

The U.N. High Commissioner for Refugees pledged to contribute U.S. $17.7 million for the relief programme; a total of £S 15,000 was received by January 1972 from the countries and organisations which responded to the U.N. Commissioner's appeal. The O.A.U. contributed £S 39,950.

The central Government in Khartoum contributed £S 750,000 while the provinces of Darfur, Kassala, Khartoum, Kordofan and Bahr el Ghazal contributed £S 24,576. Sudanese private and popular organisations and individuals contributed £S 8,634. Sudanese communities outside the Sudan (in Qatar, Abu Dhabi, Riyadh, Dubai and Saudi Arabia) contributed £S 6,068.

Contributions from international voluntary organisations amounted to £S 126,800. £S 1,850,140 was contributed to the Sudan by friendly countries and states — namely Qatar, Dubai, Saudi Arabia, Morocco, Gabon, Somalia, Cameroon, Ethiopia, Tanzania, Cyprus, Italy, the U.S.A., Britain, Egypt and Yugoslavia. In addition to this there were contributions in kind from international voluntary organisations and friendly states amounting to a value of £S 1,227,000. The total amount actually donated after the Agreement in cash and kind amounted to about £S 3 million pounds which was much less than was needed. The lack of sufficient resources in addition to the difficulties of communication presented a great problem in the resettlement and rehabilitation of the refugees.

When the conference was held in Juba at the end of January 1972 to review the situation regarding repatriation and resettlement of refugees, it became evident that although the first phase of the operation had been successful, the second phase embracing economic development would prove more challenging and difficult. The international community, in the view of many, did not respond adequately to the real needs of the situation.

The sections of the Agreement relating to the ceasefire and the incorporation of the Anya Nya in the armed forces constituted the other very important part of the Agreement, not only because they dealt directly with immediate and future peace and reconciliation, but also because of their direct relevance to those who had been fighting for seventeen years. The issues of the military and the military power were central to the whole Agreement and its smooth implementation. The Agreement had laid down that the representation of Southerners in the National Army would be in proportion to the population of the South and that the use of the armed forces would be controlled by the President of the Republic on the advice of the Regional High Executive Council. It also laid down the methods for integrating the Anya Nya into the Southern Command.

Ceasefire was established as soon as the Regional Self-Government Act was signed. Once the order was given, no shot was fired from either side and this was perhaps the most important single fact which paved the way for the full implementation of the other parts of the Agreement. Any reluctance or refusal by an individual or a group on either side to respect the ceasefire would have exposed the whole Agreement to failure and confusion. This was the real miracle.

The Joint Military Commission formed by a presidential decree in April 1972 immediately went into action. Its difficult task of incorporating '6,000 Anya Nya troops, on condition that the basic arrangements for the forces would help to regain confidence and that the steps to be taken would facilitate the integration required in the Southern Region',[11] was completed by September 1972. The Anya Nya troops were interviewed in pre-arranged camps and a medical team was appointed to assist the Commission. The agreed criteria for assimilation were: belonging to the Anya Nya, satisfactory academic qualifications, medical fitness and willingness to continue in the service. Since the Agreement laid down that 6,000 would be assimilated, it was agreed to select 2,000 from each of the three provinces. The Anya Nya forces produced for interview amounted to 15,832 in the different provinces. Of these 6,079 were assimilated into the armed forces, 1,860 into the police and prison services and 5,489 for work in the civil departments. The 2,414 medically unfit were recommended for service in the civil departments.[12]

	Total Inter- viewed	Selected for Armed Forces			Selected for Police and Prisons	Selected for Civil Service	Medically unfit but recruited for Civil Service
		Officers	N.C.O.'s	Privates			
Bahr el Ghazal	2,559	65	188	1,723	164	138	281
Equatoria	7,629	70	274	1,759	1,661	1,976	1,889
Upper Nile	4,654	65	465	1,530	35	3,375	244
Total	15,832	200	867	5,012	1,860	5,489	2,414

Officers Ranks: 1 major-general, 4 colonels, 7 lieut.-colonels, 18 majors, 57 captains, 48 lieutenants and 66 second-lieutenants.

After the Commission's work was completed, the President offered a special pension to eleven officers who had served in the Southern Corps before 1955. These included Major Taffeng and Major Paul Ali Batala. Joseph Lagu was appointed Major-General and stationed with the troops in the South.

It its final report the Commission found that the Anya Nya 'showed complete enthusiasm for the Agreement, and determination to implement it. . . . Without doubt the Anya Nya gave a good impression, joining in the efforts of the local leaders in the Southern Region and all members of the People's Armed Forces there to regain the confidence'[13] of the Southern Sudan. However, the Joint Military Commission was aware that the process of integration in the armed forces was not easy. To overcome this problem of lack of confidence, and accelerate and facilitate the process, it recommended the following measures to be accomplished in two phases.

Phase One would consist of the establishment of a good and efficient administration which would inspire confidence. The specific measures to be taken during this phase were: the selection of a good commander, construction of camps for the selected troops close to National Armed Forces centres, supervision of services such as transport and health by the National Armed Forces, joint military police, shared recreation facilities, and attachment of administrative officers and

N.C.O.s to the new units to administer and organise the work.

Phase Two would start as soon as the military and training equipment and facilities were available. The measures recommended to facilitate the integration process were: (*a*) that instructors should reside with the troops and the training programme should include lectures on civics and a campaign against tribalism and racialism; (*b*) that the officers should later be given special training at the Gabeit Infantry School and other technical military training centres in the Northern provinces; and (*c*) that the Joint Military Commission should finally recommend inter-unit and inter-provincial transfers and the re-organisation of the Southern Command with a view to creating a spirit of unity and accelerating the required process of integration.[14]

The establishment of the regional Government, the re-patriation and resettlement of refugees and displaced persons, the integration of the Anya Nya forces into the National Army, and the peace and confidence which had ultimately grown up between the North and the South were the outstanding direct results of the Addis Ababa Agreement. The year following the Agreement was, in the words of Abel Alier's address to mark the first anniversary of the Agreement, a year of 'cooling off, of receiving people, of emphasising to them that we are starting a new page in the history of the Sudan. ... For the last twelve months since the cessation of the civil strife, the nation has geared its efforts to uphold peace and to generate both collective and individual interest in creating new relations among citizens in the North and South, in emphasising the problems of the future and not to dwell on the past that had been bitter, but to draw lessons from this past to avoid future conflicts that might threaten all that goes with peace, goodwill and popular progress. Our overriding desire and concern has been to guard against . . . resumption of hostilities.'[15]

It would be fair to conclude that during the first year following the Agreement the Northern and Southern Sudanese accepted the challenges of peace. Reconciliation, continuation of peace and economic and cultural development in a united Sudan was no longer 'the heavy load of responsibility of the North'[16] but was the responsibility of the South as well.

The new Sudan Constitution which was approved in April 1973, in the making of which the Southern representatives had actively participated, was further proof of the sense of responsibility and deep desire for unity. The Southern Provinces Regional Self-Government Act 1972 had become part and parcel of the National Constitution. The adoption of the Constitution with the full participation and agreement of the Southern representatives had removed a potential source of disagreement and conflict.

But the Addis Ababa Agreement and what followed was just the beginning of a more difficult and complex task – the promotion of economic and social development in the South and the consolidation of the political unity of the Sudan, which the Agreement had set out from the beginning to achieve. Will the Sudan do another 'piece of constructive pioneer work'[17] for Africa, such as it has already done? Or will it allow itself to fail and disappoint all those individuals – Sudanese and non-Sudanese – governments and organisations who have worked so earnestly to bring about peace and unity? No one can predict the future, but the present does not create pessimism.

REFERENCES

1. Address by President Nimeiri, Omdurman, 3 March 1972.

2. K. E. Ankrah, 'Sudan, the Church and Peace', *Africa*, May 1972.

3. *Ibid.*

4. Information supplied by Mrs. Barbara Haq, Secretary of the Movement for Colonial Freedom, London.

5. *Ibid.*

6. *Ibid.*

7. *Ibid.*

8. Ministry of Foreign Affairs, *Peace and Unity in the Sudan*, Khartoum, 1973, p. 45.

9. Address by Abel Alier, Vice-President and Minister of State for Southern Affairs to the Relief and Resettlement Conference, Khartoum, 21 February 1972.

10. Appendix II.

11. Report of the Joint Military Commission, Khartoum, October 1972.

12. *Ibid.*

13. *Ibid.*

14. *Ibid.*

15. Address by Vice-President Abel Alier, Juba, 3 March 1972.

16. A. J. Toynbee, *Between Niger and Nile*, London, 1965.

17. *Ibid.*

CHAPTER VI

CONCLUSION

The quest for peace and unity in the Sudan, which had started in October 1964 and of which the foundations were laid at the Round Table Conference in March 1965 with the broad agreement contained in the resolutions of that Conference and in the 'secret minute', was finally realised through the Declaration of June 1969 and the Addis Ababa Agreement of 1972. The seven years in between were not wasted years if they are viewed in the light of the final results and achievements. Both military and non-military solutions were tried. Only when political conditions in the North and the South changed and both parties became convinced that war would not solve the problem was it possible to achieve peace.

The making of peace in the Sudan, however, differed from the making of peace in other situations. The war between the North and the South was not a war between two sovereign states. It was an 'internal' war within the same sovereign state and within the boundaries of the same country. It did not reach the stage of a civil war in the sense that all the population on both sides were involved. The Sudan's unique position in Africa, its population composition and its cultural heritages made the conflict a unique one. The outside involvement, sometimes direct and sometimes indirect and with different motivations, affected the character of the war and added to the complexity of the situation.

Since the problem of relations between North and South were unique and not similar to other problems, the making of peace and the approach to it was also unique. An African scholar has described the Addis Ababa Agreement as a landmark in the history of Africa and as important as the

Treaty of Versailles was to Europe in 1919.[1] This might be true as far as the final outcome is concerned, but the Treaty of Versailles was between sovereign states which had gone to war against each other, and the final terms were dictated by the victorious powers. The Addis Ababa Agreement was not an agreement between sovereign states; nor was it dictated by a victorious group on a defeated one.

The similarity between the two lies in the fact that both were concerned with the problem of nationalities, minority groups and future relations within states. The Versailles Treaty ended the war in Europe and attempted to fix the principles on which future peace in Europe was to be founded; the Addis Ababa Agreement ended the war in the Sudan and attempted to lay the principles on which future peace within African states with similar problems was to be founded.

As a result of the Versailles Treaty, new attitudes and new relations developed within Europe and between Europe and the outside world. The Addis Ababa Agreement created new attitudes within the Sudan and between the Sudan and other countries, especially in Africa.

Because it was a landmark in the history of the Sudan and Africa, it was welcomed with great enthusiasm. This was justified enthusiasm because, 'for a long time before that, the news coming from Africa was disheartening and disappointing'[2] to the friends of Africa. The pessimists and cynics were confounded. An example of these was Arnold Toynbee, who wrote in 1969 in his introduction to Oliver Albino's *The Sudan − a Southern Viewpoint*: 'The facts presented in the book do not offer hope of a speedy or happy issue out of the present impasse.'[3] He almost suggested that no solution would be found because 'this would require a degree of good will and wisdom that is very rare today.'[4] What seemed impossible in 1969 was achieved in less than three years. The solution, on the other hand, was neither imposed from outside 'by great powers, nor arranged by disinterested international organizations.'[5] In this way it was not only a Sudanese triumph but also an African one.

First, successful peace-making required an understanding of the problem in its various and true dimensions. Secondly, it needed action in both the making of the decisions and in implementing them. Thirdly, the solutions for the problem could not have been read in textbooks on war and peace. No books dealing with a situation like that of the Sudan existed. They could only be found and reached by those involved in the events.

The negotiators on both sides were faced from the beginning with tremendous problems. On the Northern side, the Government in Khartoum had not, until then, been receiving firm mass support. The leadership of the traditional political parties continued to oppose the régime. The communists, in spite of the fact that they were originally the promoters of the idea of autonomy for the South, depicted the negotiations as a deal with the pro-western elements among the Southerners; the abortive *coup d'état* of July 1971 and the events which followed as a result had thrown them deep into the opposition camp. The pro-Arab elements were suspicious that the exercise would push the Sudan away from its alliance in the Arab world and into new alliances in Africa. The Muslim Brothers, who advocate an Islamic constitution for the Sudan, opposed any settlement that would not recognize this principle.

The Southern side had its own and special problems. Aggrey Jaden and Gordon Muortat, who both had large support in the Southern political movement, refused from the beginning to take part in the negotiations. Others opposed the negotiations because they did not include the question of separation. The 'anti-Arab' elements mistrusted the Arab North and would not be convinced that there was a new policy and a change of heart in the North. Some missionaries who had been actively involved in the problem, such as Father Ferrari, also opposed the negotiations. The Israelis, who for a number of years had supplied weapons and training for the South, and who looked upon the Southern problem largely in the context of the conflict in the Middle East, were active in their efforts to sabotage the negotiations. These factors, together with the bitterness and mistrust created during seventeen years of conflict, added to the complexity of the situation and of the task facing the negotiators. But only when both sides recognised these difficulties and complexities was it possible to go a step further.

It is true that it had taken a long period of preparation, more than two years, since the negotiations were started in 1970 until the final talks were held. It is also true that it had taken a comparatively short period, about four months, to arrange the Round Table Conference. But the objectives of the Round Table Conference, its nature and the conditions in which it was convened differed from those of the Addis Ababa Agreement. The problem of the Southern Sudan had not assumed the same dimensions in 1965 as it had done by 1971. The political set-up in the country at the time of the Round Table Conference differed from that during 1969—72.

The meetings at Addis Ababa, unlike those of the Round Table Conference, were closed except to delegates, advisers and observers. No press and radio reporters were admitted. No aggressive speeches were directed to the public, as at Khartoum in 1965. The fact that the negotiations were conducted inside closed doors contributed to the frankness of the discussions. There were no inhibitions. Although agreement had already been reached on the principles and some of the details, the negotiations were long and heated. Sometimes it seemed as if no solution could be found. But as human beings, the two sides could not afford to continue disagreeing on every issue or point for a long time. Ordinary human courtesy in such conditions normally prevails, and this is what really happened at Addis Ababa. Neither side shouted against the other, as happened at the Round Table Conference.

On the other hand, no one on either side could afford a failure of the negotiations after all the effort and persuasion that had gone into the preparations for the talks. The political future of everyone who took part depended to some extent on the talks succeeding. Failure would have been disastrous for both sides.

There were no rules of procedure to discuss and spend time over, as at the Round Table Conference. The delegates had little time to relax and prolong the discussions. The feeling of urgency prompted all of them not to waste time on minor issues.

The choice of Addis Ababa as the meeting place was appropriate. The decision by the Government not to insist on Khartoum, as had been suggested by some, because of considerations of sovereignty, was wise. The Southern leaders who were reluctant to take part in the negotiations would have refused if Khartoum had been insisted upon as the meeting place. Those who refused to take part unless separation was agreed upon in advance would have found a justification for their opposition. The bitterness, misunderstanding and lack of confidence which had been built up over seventeen years would have made it very difficult for the Southern leaders to agree to hold the meetings in Khartoum. The choice of Addis Ababa made their job much easier as far as their supporters were concerned.

On the other hand, as Khartoum was disqualified, Addis Ababa seemed the most appropriate place for such negotiations. It is the seat of the Organization of African Unity, and reconciliation has become part of the image and tradition of the city. The general atmosphere and climate of opinion there was not hostile to the Sudan; indeed, the previous two years had witnessed a better understanding and more friendly relations between the two countries. Furthermore, the political leaders of the Southern Sudan looked upon Ethiopia as a country friendly to their cause: it was a Christian country where many Southern refugees and some of the Southern leaders lived and enjoyed comparative freedom of movement.

The only other possible city was Geneva, but this would have given the impression of internationalizing the problem. It was a European city where some of the churches and voluntary organizations involved in the problem were active. Any other place outside Africa would not therefore have been appropriate.

In addition, the Emperor of Ethiopia was seen by many African leaders as the father of African unity and by others as the wise man of Africa. He seemed the most suitable Head of an African state to mediate when necessary. He knew the Sudan well and was friendly with the country. He had also reacted positively to the new Sudan's policy of friendship initiated in 1969.

The negotiations were carried on by those who carried great weight on both sides. The Sudan Government representatives were headed by Abel Alier, the Vice-President, a Southerner with support in the South who was respected and trusted in the North; also present were the Minister of the Interior, Foreign Affairs, Local Government and Public Service. All the four were influential in the Cabinet and close to President Nimeiri. They were not only directly involved in the making of policies, but also in their execution. The Minister of Public Service, Abdel Rahman Abdalla, had had first-hand experience of the problem while a member of the Secretariat of the Round Table Conference and later in the Twelve-Man Committee. Both Brigadier Mirghani Suleiman and Colonel Kamal Abashar had first-hand knowledge of the problem by virtue of their positions in the Army.

The representation of the Southern Sudan Liberation Movement came from those who had the most support among the Anya Nya and the Southern politicians outside the Sudan. Colonel Frederick Brian Maggot was the second man after General Lagu in the Anya Nya hierarchy. Mading deGarang and Lawrence Wol Wol were General Lagu's special representatives in Europe. The first was involved in the preparatory talks and was responsible for the editing of *Grass Curtain* in London. Lawrence Wol Wol, who participated in the Round Table Conference, had been responsible for the publication of the *Voice of the Southern Sudan* and had close contacts with the church and voluntary organizations in Europe and America. Ezboni Mondiri Gwonza, a veteran politician, ex-M.P. and in 1964 Minister of Communications, was one of the most active politicans in the South. Oliver Albino was known for his extreme anti-Arab and anti-North points of view. The Rev. Paul Puot represented the Church elements. The different attitudes and political points of view, as well as the different factions, were well represented.

It is true that neither side was elected by those whom it claimed to represent. It is also true that neither side had the 'legal' mandate required in other situations. However, this was not a negotiation between two sovereign states. The Government of General Nimeiri was not 'legal' or constitutional in the sense of being an elected government; it had come to power through a military revolution and had acquired its legality from its ability to continue to exist and rule the country. Nor was the Southern Sudan Liberation Movement a legal entity. It was an organization of those who rebelled against the legally constituted Government of the Sudan; its 'legality' derived from its ability to continue to exist and fight. After all, the final agreement when closely examined is based on the discussions, findings and resolutions of the 'legally' constituted régimes before 1969. The resolutions of the Round Table Conference, the recommendations of the Twelve-Man Committee and the findings of the Political Parties Conference were the basis of the Agreement; so if there is any issue of legality it should be viewed in this context and not in the context of legal representation of individuals.

Besides the delegates from both sides, very few outsiders took part. Few observers at Addis Ababa actually participated in the discussions. Nabiyelul Kifle represented Emperor Haile Selassie personally, and provided liaison between the negotiators and the Emperor when this was necessary. The representatives of the World Council of Churches and the All Africa Council of Churches were as keen as the negotiators for a settlement to be reached. The World Council of Churches was becoming ever more involved in the political problems of Africa, but its involvement was being made in a new spirit. The old attitude of viewing the problem as religious and therefore of being hostile to the North was being replaced by a new sympathetic attitude; thus the involvement of the World Council in the negotiations was a test of its new policy and attitude – hence its keenness for the success of the negotiations.

The fact that K. E. Ankrah and Burgess Carr, the mediators (in place of a chairman), were both Africans – the first from Ghana and the second from Liberia – contributed to their success in their role. Notwithstanding the fact that they both represented Church organizations, they were accepted by the Northern representatives. Their 'Africa-ness' was more influential than their Church connections – hence their acceptability.

Samuel Athi Bwogo, who represented the Sudan Council

of Churches, had been actively involved in the preparatory talks. He had previously travelled to Geneva and to East Africa to brief the Church organizations and advise them on the different issues involved in the problem. He had received the Church representatives when they were visiting Khartoum and provided liaison between them and the Sudan Government. He was at home with the representatives of the World Council of Churches and the All Africa Conference of Churches, and with the Northern and Southern Sudanese representatives. That he was a Southern Sudanese himself was an added asset.

The only outsider with no past involvement in the Southern problem, direct or indirect, was Sir Dingle Foot, a former British Labour M.P. He was brought to Addis Ababa by the Southern side to act as constitutional adviser. He was not actually present in the meetings, but his advice was given whenever it was needed.

Before the Agreement and its implications for the future are examined we should try to answer questions which are often asked: why was the Addis Ababa Agreement reached at that particular time? Could it not have been postponed until a time when the political and constitutional organs were established?

To answer these questions would require inside knowledge of the situation among the rebels and in the Government circles. But from the little information we have, certain factors which determined the reaching of an agreement at that point can be identified.

First, both sides were by then convinced that no military solution was possible or in sight. In spite of the fact that the army was better equipped and better trained, and was often successful in destroying or capturing some of the rebel camps, it did not succeed in eliminating all their hostile activities.

The rebels, on the other hand, realized that their guerrilla warfare would only succeed if it were supported by the local population and if a continuous supply of arms were guaranteed. But this was not the case. The population, which had been suffering from the war for seventeen years, found

itself caught between the two sides. Many preferred to desert
their villages and go to the towns, or flee the country. There
was a shortage of arms. The neighbouring countries through
which the arms were smuggled were reluctant to help because
of the Sudan's new policy of friendly relations with its
neighbours, which had been developed since 1969. The visits
made by President Nimeiri to the neighbouring countries
with a view to explaining the problem and the solutions
suggested resulted in the decline of official support given to
the rebels.

Both sides, therefore, were convinced that no military
solution was possible or in sight.

Secondly, the military operations in the South were a
continuous drain on the resources of the North. The
Government, which was committed to a policy of economic
and social development, was finding it more difficult to fulfil
this task while the war continued. The rate of economic and
social growth in both the North and the South suffered
because of the war. At the same time, aid from other
countries for economic and social development was not
forthcoming. Western European countries, traditional sources
for assistance, were not enthusiastic in helping the Sudan out
of its difficulties as long as the war continued. The instability
caused by the war in both the North and the South reduced
the potential of aid from these countries and from international organizations. The solution of the Southern problem, the Government hoped, would remove some of the
restrictions on aid and assistance.

Thirdly, due to the new policy towards the South, more
and more Southerners were convinced that there was no
alternative to the cessation of hostilities and the establishment of peace. At least, they argued, the new policy should
be given a trial. The Association of Southern Intellectuals was
active both inside and outside the Sudan in advocating this.
The number of refugees returning from outside increased.
More and more younger Southerners educated outside the
Sudan were persuaded that the new policy was genuine. The
rebels were therefore finding that the support they used to
receive among the Southerners, and which they hoped to
increase, was in part decreasing. Although the rebels were

united under the new leadership of Colonel Lagu, divisions and disagreements still persisted among them and this was a source of the weakness in the movement.

Fourthly, the approaches made by the World Council of Churches to the Southern political leaders, which began in May 1971, were intensified during the following months. In these approaches and contacts the main issues discussed were the questions of peace. A general consensus of opinion on the desirability of peace was established.

Fifthly, the abortive *coup d'état* of July 1971 and the resulting changes in policies, government structure and personnel removed the doubts which existed in the minds of many Southerners about the genuineness of the régime's intentions towards the South. The policy of giving priority to the establishment of democratic socialist organizations before the implementation of the declaration of June 1969 was no longer valid.

Lastly, the appointment of Abel Alier as Vice-President and Minister for Southern Affairs in August 1971 accelerated the whole operation of peace; he enjoyed confidence in the North and among a large number of Southern Sudanese inside the Sudan, also among the leadership of the rebels. Details of a draft act on self-government was worked out by a Committee of the Sudanese Socialist Union working closely with a group of Southern intellectuals.

These were the main factors which promoted action to reach peace on both sides at that time. The hesitation on both sides — more on the Southern side than the Northern — was overcome, and the obstacles in the path for peace were cleared.

It is often asked whether the Agreement was the result of a new foreign policy of less involvement in Arab issues and more involvement in African issues.

It would be fair to say that since May 1969 the Government set out to promote its image in both the Arab and African countries. Since historically relations with the Arab countries, especially Egypt, were closer than those with other countries in Africa, it was natural for the Government to seek closer and more friendly relations with its neighbours to the North. The May revolution was partly inspired by the Egyptian revolution. The Sudanese nationalist movement was traditionally close to that of Egypt; Sudanese nationalists received support from the Egyptian nationalists during their struggle for independence.

The countries neighbouring the Sudan to the South, East and West had limited contact with it before and after their independence; the nationalist movements in these countries did not have close relations with the nationalist movement in the Sudan. Even with the Southern Sudan there was little contact politically or culturally. Except for the relatively small movement of people between Uganda, for example, and the Southern Sudan, and the fact that Christian missionaries operated in both areas, there was little cultural contact. Southern Sudanese nationalists before independence did not look southwards for inspiration.

It was natural therefore for the Sudan, during the post-independence period, to continue to look to the North. This implied involvement in the political issues of the Arab world. As a result, its foreign policy became orientated towards the problems of the Arab world which were essentially problems of Arab nationalism, the political unity of the Arab countries, the Palestine problem and the fight against foreign – and especially Western – domination. The degree of involvement was not the same all the time. Although this differed from one régime to another and from one political party to another, the Sudan's engagement in the Arab world was accepted as a fact. Its membership in the Arab League further promoted this involvement.

African issues and problems presented themselves with less intensity and urgency than those of the Arab world. The Sudan's neighbours to the West and South became independent only after 1960, and the Organization of African Unity came into being in 1963. The Sudan became a member of the O.A.U. and through this its involvement in the problems of African countries and African issues began. The issues and problems in Africa immediately after independence were not the same as those facing the Arab world: their immediate problems related to laying the foundations for economic and political co-operation within the continent, the peaceful solution of conflicts between African states and the promotion of support for the liberation movements against foreign domination. But although the Sudan, as a member of the O.A.U., became involved in its affairs, this involvement was much less than its involvement in the issues of the Arab world. As long as the problems of the latter were more pressing and those of the African world less so, its involvement in the Arab world was likely to be more apparent.

The new policy towards the Southern problem manifested in the declaration of July 1969 was the foundation of a new emphasis and direction in the Sudan's foreign policy. As more emphasis was placed on the need and urgency to solve the Southern problem, the need and urgency to improve the Sudan's relations with its neighbours and its fellow-members of the O.A.U. became apparent. Its involvement in the problems and issues of Africa increased. This contributed to the solution of the Southern problem.

These new directions in foreign policy were not, however, viewed as necessarily leading to less engagement in the Arab world. On the contrary, the policy-makers and their advisers saw the new African relations and the new directions following from them as complementary to the emphasis on relations with the Arab world and in no way mutually contradictory; they felt that the promotion of one would strengthen and help the promotion of the other.

The Sudan's seemingly reduced involvement in the problems and issues of the Arab world following 1972 can not be explained by the signing of the Addis Ababa Agreement. There were other factors, the chief being the disunity and conflict in the Arab world, into which the Sudan preferred not to be drawn; also the Sudan's insistence to give priority to the solution of its own political and economic problems.

Related to this issue of involvement with the Arab World and Africa is the issue of the Sudan's Arabism and Africanism. The question has been discussed at length by other writers.[6] Whenever the problem of the Southern Sudan is discussed, the question is raised whether the Sudan is African or Arab. The very asking of the question implies a conflict between the two and that the Sudan, in its search for unity, has to identify itself with one or other of them.

The terms 'Arabism' and 'Africanism' are relatively new in

the vocabulary of Sudanese political life. The British, on the reconquest of the Sudan, regarded the country, for historical and political reason, as an Arab colony. In laying the foundations of its administration and educational system they were inspired by their experiences in India and the Arab world, especially Egypt. The educational policies and systems practised were similar to those of Egypt, and Egyptian teachers were employed to teach in the Sudan's British-controlled schools. The Sudan's orientation was more towards Egypt than toward Britain's colonies in Africa. The early Sudanese nationalists were more orientated towards Cairo than any other place. Ali Abdel Latif and his associates in the White League Society in 1924 identified the Sudan with Egypt, and advocated the unity of the two countries. This identification was based on political rather than on racial considerations, and those political parties in the Northern Sudan which had advocated in the past the unity of Egypt and the Sudan thought also in political terms. The unity of the Nile valley was to them a matter of political expediency. They recognised common elements between the Northern Sudan and other countries in the Arab world: namely, the Arabic language and Islam. They also recognised that Egypt enjoyed a special position in relation to the Arab world. In addition to the two factors of religion and language, those of history, geography, the Nile, intermarriage and migration provided the basis on which the special relationship rested. Even those who opposed the unity of the Nile valley did not deny these factors.

The Northern Sudanese generally identified themselves with the Arab world through identifying themselves with Egypt. Egypt was the window through which they viewed the outside world.

O. Aguda writes as follows: 'Before the explosive emergence of political consciousness in post-war black Africa, "enlightened" Arab Sudanese looked almost exclusively to Arab culture and the Arab world for their political aspirations and identification. It was natural that they should do so, since they were undoubtedly more Arab than African in their culture. ... Besides, the Africans in the Southern Sudan, who were among the most backward peoples on the continent, could hardly inspire their Arab compatriots with any desire to identify with Africa.'[7]

Only after independence in 1956, and when Arab nationalism under Jamal Abdel Nasser assumed its new dimensions, did the question of the Sudan's relations with the Arab world and its identity become an issue in Sudanese political life. This new Arab nationalism, which stands not only for Arab unity but also 'as a shield and protection against imperialism and as an instrument of victory over Israel'[8] and is regarded as a movement of emancipation 'from the political interference of western powers, whether visible or invisible, from the federal spirit and mentality of the indigenous society',[9] did not mean the same old and traditional nationalism. It acquired a new orientation towards socialism. The alliance between Arab nationalism and socialism received increasing support from the educated youth in the Arab world. Those Northern Sudanese who identified the Sudan with the Arab world thought of Arabism in these new terms of Arab nationalism more than in terms of race.

In the mean time, the issue of identification with Africa did not arise in their minds. Until then, all the countries of Africa except Ethiopia and Liberia had been under colonial rule. Ghana became independent in 1957 – one year after the Sudan. African nationalism was thus concerned in the first place with political independence. The concepts of Pan-Africanism and African unity did not dominate the political thinking of African leaders until the 1960s. The nationalist movement in the Sudan had little contact with the independence movements in Africa. The policies of the colonial powers, the difficulties of communication and the language problems were barriers which made such contacts difficult. They had no contact with the Pan-Africanist movement in its early years. The Sudan continued to look northwards, especially to Egypt.

When the concepts of Pan-Africanism and African unity assumed new dimensions under Kwame Nkrumah, and the Sudan became a member of the O.A.U. and thereby involved in African affairs, the relations of the Sudan with the African world became a subject of discussion and an issue in Sudanese politics. The problem of the Southern Sudan was at the centre of this relation. The Southern Sudanese considered themselves different from the Northern Sudan, as from Egypt and the Arab world, in terms of race and language. The political leadership among the Southern Sudanese identified itself more with African problems and inspiration than with those of the Arabs. The identification here, like that of the Northern Sudanese with Egypt, was with East Africa more than with Africa as a whole; the minority Christian élite argued that there were more common factors between them and their counterparts in East Africa than with the Arab world. These factors are racial and cultural. People from the same tribes live on both sides of the borders of the Sudan with Uganda, Kenya, Zaire and Ethiopia. Thousands of Southern Sudanese refugees have lived in these countries. The majority of the political leaders in these regions are Christian and English-speaking.

The identification with East Africa and, through that, with Africanism, like the identification of the Northern Sudan with Egypt and, through that, with the Arab world, was in the first place due to political expediency. They were concerned with the relations of the South with the North and not with the militant anti-imperialist concepts of Pan-Africanism or African unity. As the neighbouring countries became more involved, directly or indirectly, in the Southern problem, the issue of the Sudan's identification with the Arab world and Africanism became an issue in Sudanese politics.

The cold war and the conflict in the Middle East had contributed to this identification exercise. Identification with militant Arab nationalism and especially with Egypt was in fact an identification with anti-Western and anti-Israeli politics. Identification with Pan-Africanism did not, at the time, give the same degree of inspiration as the anti-Western or anti-Israeli policies. In 1966 Israel had diplomatic relations with twenty-nine African countries. Her relations with the countries of East Africa, especially Ethiopia, Uganda and Kenya, were close, and support and assistance were also given to the rebel movement in the Southern Sudan. The end of the cold war and of the conflict in the Middle East will remove some of the factors which have contributed to the misleading suggestion that Pan-Arabism and Pan-Africanism are contradictory.

In fact Pan-Arabism and Arab aspirations are not contradictory to Pan-Africanism and African aspirations. The majority of those who describe themselves as Arabs — 60 per cent — live in Africa. They are involved in the problems of the continent as much as those who describe themselves as Africans. The past divisions between Arab Africa and Non-Arab Africa, between Islamic Africa and non-Islamic Africa, between Black Africa and non-Black Africa and between Africa north of the Sahara and Africa south of the Sahara are disappearing fast. New concepts of Pan-Africanism and African unity and co-operation are replacing those concepts which have, in the past, led to conflicts. Pan-Africanism can hardly be distinguished today from revolutionary Pan-Arabism.

Ali Mazrui, in his exposition of the Sudan's multiple marginality, states:

> The Arabs constitute the most important link between . . . Africa and Asia. The Sudan constitutes the most important contact between Arab Africa and Negro Africa. There is first the very phenomenon of racial mixture and intermarriage in the northern parts of the Sudan, coupled with the fact that a large population of Arab Sudanese are Arabized Negroes, rather than ethnically Semitic, and for many of them the Arab-ness is a cultural acquisition rather than a racial heredity.[10]

He also writes that the Sudan

> . . . serves comparable functions between other segments of the total African pattern. One could see the Sudan as a bridge between Arabic speaking and English speaking Africa, between Christian Africa and Muslim Africa, between the Africa of the homogenized mass nation states of the future and the Africa of the deep ethnic cleavage of the present, and finally between West Africa as a cultural unit and Eastern Africa.[11]

Other communities in Africa, which have been quoted as examples of an Arab-African unity, although to a lesser degree, are Somalia, Chad, Niger, Mali, Nigeria, Senegal and

Mauritania.[12] Thus the politics of Afro-Arab cultural conflict and harmony are not exclusively the burden or concern of the Sudan; but in the case of the Sudan they have been magnified, and in some cases exaggerated. A number of African countries which have elected to contain and try to harmonize the diverse elements within their own boundaries rather than allow the fragmentation of the territory into isolated tribal entities, have experienced ethnic cultural conflicts in the same way as the Sudan.

'The fascination of the Sudan', writes Ali Mazrui, 'lies in her profound intermediacy as she compulsively absorbs into her being a diversity of traits. Parts of Africa which are otherwise vastly different have been known to experience a moment of self-recognition as they cast their eyes on the Sudan.'[13]

The Addis Ababa Agreement has tried, through a new approach to peace, to lay the foundations of a new constitutional and political structure which would promote national integration in the Sudan. The Sudan's Permanent Constitution, adopted in May 1973 (one year after the Addis Ababa Agreement) identified the Sudan as 'part of both Arab and African entities',[14] and declared Arabic the official language of the state. Article 9 of the Constitution recognizes both the Islamic law and custom as the main sources of legislation, while the personal matters of non-Muslims would be governed by their personal laws.[15] These provisions – together with Article 16 of the Constitution, which gives recognition to Islam and Christianity as religions of the Sudan – makes it incumbent on the State 'not to impose any restrictions on the citizens or communities on the grounds of religious faith'.[17] The adoption of these articles in the new Constitution ended the debate, at least for the time being, and legalized the entity of the country in relation to the Arab and African world.

But what about the future?

The most important aspect of the Addis Ababa Agreement, besides ending the seventeen-year-old conflict between the North and the South, and the turning of an outlawed secessionist movement into a politically respectable move-

ment committed to the unity of the Sudan, is the establishment of regional self-government in the South. The Regional
Self-Government Act 1972 excluded both federal and centralized systems as patterns of government and administration capable of promoting national integration. Federalism,
whereby powers at all levels are divided between the centre
and regions, would not have been capable of promoting
national integration in the Sudan. It might be a sound system
of government in other countries such as Australia or
Switzerland, but in these countries each of the communities
seeking unity has reached an advanced stage in nationhood.
Their 'small' nations which constitute the big nation are
equal. Because they have reached an advanced stage of
economic and cultural development, the danger of disintegration arising from political tension is minimal. In those
countries where the communities have not yet reached the
stage of full nationhood, the danger of disintegration under a
federal system arises from the fact that the loyalty of the
individual or the community is to the region in the first place
rather than to the state as a whole.

Federalism, on the other hand, is an expensive system
which poor and developing nations cannot afford. Their
meagre resources will be heavily taxed by the additional
expenses which arise from the duplication of organs of
government and administration and the large number of
personnel employed. Efficiency and the decision-making
process are hampered by the complicated legislative and
administrative laws and procedures.

Even in countries where federalism has been accepted at
one stage of their development as the sound system of
government, the tendency is for more centralization. The
need to plan the economy at the national level, to reduce the
costs of administration, to co-ordinate the social services and
to co-operate at the regional and international level, have all
contributed to the promotion of the concept of centralization in place of federation.

Federalism, in its classical sense, does not therefore suit
the conditions of the Sudan. Rafia Hassan Ahmed writes:

> The arguments of short financial resources, scarcity of
> educated and skilled cadre, and the divergence of already

distorted national loyalties, are all applicable to the Sudan case. Federation will definitely weaken the already weak Sudanese government. It will create sentiments of selfishness in the federal regions, and this in turn will obstruct national solidarity as well as the efforts for mobilizing all the resources for the development of the depressed areas and the other parts of the country as well. The relationships between northerners and southerners are weak and lack mutual confidence and federation will further deteriorate these relations. Granting federal constitutional powers, which are not easily revocable, and in most cases cannot be controlled except by military force, may lead to serious political problems between the federal government and the unit governments and this may worsen the situation in the south rather than solve the problem.[18]

On the other hand, the centralized system of government, where all powers are in the hands of the central government and there are no duplications of administrative organs, might seem the most suitable system in developing countries where financial resources and qualified personnel are lacking. This is not, however, the case of all countries: centralization has proved itself unsuited to the conditions of the Sudan. 'Centralization', writes Rafia Hassan Ahmed,

> ... had failed to secure stability to the Sudanese society or to solve the southern problem. In fact strong centralization during the first military regime had aggravated the southern problem to the extent that the Anya Nya military secessionist movement emerged together with its active political movement in exile. This new dimension of the problem showed itself because the southerners had no opportunity to assert their identity or administer their own affairs.[19]

Thus in these countries where 'ethnic, religious and socio-cultural pluralism has a strong grip among the people',[20] centralization, like federalism, can promote disintegration.

Regionalism, where some of the powers are exclusively invested in the central government while others are exclusively delegated to the regions, seems to be the system most suitable to the conditions of the Sudan as far as North-South relations are concerned. The system of regional self-government avoids some but not all the duplications, complications and large expenses associated with the federal system. On the other hand, it avoids the faults of the centralized system where all the powers are concentrated in the centre and there is little participation by the region in decision-making.

It is not enough, however, to agree and accept regional self-government as the most suitable system for the Sudan; the agreement and the system established are no more than laying the foundations for national integration. What is important is to see that the system works and the difficulties are overcome.

It should be recognized in the first place that the physical environment in the South, the political institutions and the social systems of the tribes are not conducive to easy change and hence to national integration. The swamps and forests and the lack of a good communications system within the region and with the North and the outside world have contributed in the past to the isolation of the different peoples from each other and from the outside world. The people of the South, 'particularly the Nilotics, have been characterized as conservative and hostile to change, especially to any change that is forced upon them.'[21] It has been suggested that, although the resistance of the other tribes to outside influence and change did not equal that of the Nilotics, 'hardly any could be classified, for example, with the Ibo of Nigeria in the welcome they extended to newcomers and to new ideas.'[22] 'Within the same structure of every tribe', writes Rudolph Ibrahim Samuel,

> ... there are traditions, customs and beliefs that impede the economic system. The social institution prohibits the effective utilization of factors of production for the sake of development. ... Most of the tribes do not react in an expected way to the stimulus of incentive. They pay more attention to the present and immediate gain that they can attain rather than to the distant future. Once the goal that they are striving for is achieved, they lack the desire to continue work. This is a typical example of the backward sloping supply curve of effort which characterizes most of the developing countries.[23]

For most of the people, political consciousness does not extend beyond the level of the tribe. The concept of loyalty to the Southern Sudan or to the Sudan as a whole scarcely exists except in the minds of those educated Southern Sudanese who have the opportunity to travel outside their tribal areas. In some cases this loyalty does not extend even to all parts of the tribe. For example, Dinka living outside their own sub-tribal centre are looked upon by other Dinka 'as foreigners and probably would not undertake a journey into another Dinka sub-tribal area without guarantees of safe-conduct.'[24] The Nuer and the Zande may be a little different, but they exhibit the same characteristics.[25]

Although the political systems of the South may exist 'at a very low order of integration',[26] a wider group consciousness, extending beyond the tribe, has recently developed among educated Southerners. It is this consciousness which stimulated political dissent. The peace obtained in the South and the establishment of regional self-government will further stimulate loyalty to the region among a wider group of Southerners. The development and promotion of national loyalty among the Southerners will be a long process. The successful establishment of national institutions, and the active participation of the Southerners in these institutions, will stimulate national loyalty and unity.

For the successful achievement of this objective, it is necessary to give priority to the past causes of conflict. One such cause is economic equality: the backwardness of the South and the unequal economic growth of the two parts of the country. Economic development in the past was concentrated in the North and the Southerners had few opportunities in commerce and trade. With the exception of the Zande Scheme, the British administration did little to develop the potentialities of the South. The Malut Scheme, the Wau Fruit Canning Factory and the extension of the railway to Wau were the major works done in the post-independence period. Because of the war the economic gap between the North and the South increased. Today the South contributes little to the Sudan's exports and accounts only for about 11 per cent of the total national output. 'In terms of economic development' writes Othwan Dak, 'the South is far behind the North no matter what criteria are used.'[27]

The more favourable economic position of the North and the coming of peace to the country will not automatically lead to the closure of the economic gap. Special measures will have to be taken to achieve greater equality in economic development and growth. The regional government has been invested, according to the Addis Ababa Agreement, with the right to levy duties and taxes and to receive contributions from the Central Government.[28] The region will have its own special economic planning board and its own special development budget. But these measures alone are not sufficient to generate economic growth and remove economic inequalities. Investment and taxation policies, if not well conceived, may perpetuate divisions and inequalities. Thus a new economic policy is needed, different from the traditional policies and especially designed to promote both integration and growth.

Relevant to this is the problem of transport and communications between the North and the South and within the South itself. Like economic development, transportation and communication services were less developed in the South than in to the North. The transport and communication systems were developed during the early years of the Condominium administration to meet military needs, and were later extended to the areas of agricultural production. Very little has been done in the extension of these facilities since independence. The Southern Sudan, therefore, remained in physical isolation. The physical barriers created by the Sudd, the great distance and high costs of transport discouraged intercourse with the North.

Specialists warned in the past about this alarming situation because of its economic and political implications.[29] What is more alarming is the fact that while the Sudan has been cited as an example of an 'immobile nation',[30] little has been done to review the system in the light of the needs of national unity.

The promotion of communications and telecommunications and of air and inter-regional river transport has been vested, according to the Addis Ababa Agreement, in the central Government, while the construction of roads in accordance with the national plans and programmes has been vested in the regional Government. Since the development of communication and transport systems are essential elements in reducing the mutual isolation of the two regions, and in increasing the potentialities of interaction through mixing together, their development should be given priority.

The same can be said about the mass media. Radio Omdurman is not often heard in the South. There is not a single printed newspaper in the whole region. The *Nile Mirror*, published in Khartoum and printed in English, hardly reaches the Southern Sudan. The radio and the newspaper, like transport, are important elements in the process of integration.

Other areas which have given rise to conflict in the past are education, language and religion. The inequality in educational attainment between the North and the South is a direct result of the educational policies of the Condominium administration. The provision of education was entrusted to the missionary societies, which did not provide more than they could afford; what they did provide accorded to their own needs and policies, which did not necessarily coincide with the needs of the Southerners. Educational policies differed from one missionary society to another. The emphasis was on apostolization more than on education as such. The gap in educational attainment increased in the post-independence period because of the conflict and the closure of many schools. This deficiency in educational facilities led in the past not only to widespread illiteracy in the South compared to the North, but also to very few Southerners attaining high posts in the Civil Service.

Not only were the educational opportunities limited, but the quality of education in the North and the South was different: missionary education imparted different values from schools administered by the Government. The steps taken after independence with a view to removing these differences and to integrating the two systems were not always welcomed either by the missionaries or the Southern élite. That education is a major factor in national integration is a recognized fact needing no elaboration; the provision of more educational opportunities for the Southerners and the imparting by the schools of values which promote tolerance and loyalty to the nation and not to the tribe should therefore be given priority in the educational planning of the country. While educational planning has been entrusted to the central Government, the establishment and administration of state schools at all levels has been vested, according to the Addis Ababa Agreement, in the regional Government. This is to be done in accordance with the national plan for education and economic and social development. Parents are, however, guaranteed the right to have their children and those under their care educated in accordance with their choice.

This implies that private schools could be established to educate children not necessarily in accordance with the national needs and interests. The Catholic Church in the Sudan has always insisted on such a right, and its application of this right could lead to problems in the future. The days when western missionary societies could contribute positively to African education have gone. Countries such as the Sudan engaged in nation-building place their objectives at risk by permitting outside agencies to run and administer schools for their nationals. This applies equally to the North, where such schools are provided. This is not to say that some of these schools are not better equipped and have better qualified teachers than the state schools.

In order to avoid misunderstandings on this issue of education and with a view to using education effectively as an instrument of national integration, it is essential that the educational planning specified in the agreement should be immediately worked out. Such a plan should take into consideration not only the removal of inequalities, but also the manpower needs of the whole country and the creation of Sudanese citizens with loyalty to the nation and not the region. It should aim at imparting those values and concepts which would promote unity. Such values and concepts are today lacking in Sudan's education.

The reform of the system should include, among other things, the promotion of the teaching of Arabic in the South and of one of the Southern languages to the children in the North. Language, like education, has been one of the areas of contention between the North and the South. Although the Sudan is a multilingual country with more than 100 separate languages, Arabic is the dominant language spoken by about

51.5 per cent of the population. The next largest language group is the Nilotic group of languages (18 per cent) spoken by the Dinka, Nuer and Shilluk. In the North, non-Arabic languages spoken by the Beja, Nubians and Nuba are spoken by 12.3 per cent. Nilo-Hamitic languages such as Bari are spoken by 4.6 per cent and Sudanic languages, chiefly Zande, by 4.7 per cent. Darfurian languages, chiefly the Fur, are spoken by 5.3 per cent and West African languages by 3.5 per cent. There is no single Southern language which could be classified as dominant.

The use of Arabic has been associated in the past with Islam and the Northern people. British policy during the Condominium discouraged its use for the purposes of administration and instead promoted the use of English. The missionary societies used English as the language of com-munication in both churches and schools, and at the time of independence there was an in-built resistance to the use of Arabic in the administration or in the schools. The unifica-tion of the systems of education after independence, the increase in migration from the South to the North by those seeking employment, and the general increase in contact between Northerners and Southerners, especially in the urban areas, has however led to an increase in the use of Arabic as a language of communication. Its use has increased more than expected during the years of independence because of the new policies and practices in the South.

In the past the educated Southerners looked upon Arabic as a foreign language and preferred to communicate in English, although the latter is more foreign than Arabic. As long as the conflict continued, Arabic was associated with the Arab world and Islam. Their rejection of the North implied also rejection of the Arabic language and its use as a language of communication.

These dimensions of the language problem have been recognized by the Addis Ababa Agreement. Article 6 of the Agreement states that 'Arabic shall be the official language for the Sudan, and English the principal language for the Southern region, without prejudice to the use of any other language or languages which may serve a practical necessity for the efficient and expeditious discharge of executive and administrative functions of the region.'[31] National integration cannot, however, be accelerated if English continues to be accorded a principal place and the Southern languages are accorded a minor position; In the process of national integration, English cannot play the same role as Arabic and a Southern language.

English could be a useful language for communication between the educated groups in the North and the South; indeed it is useful for many other purposes. But there is a need to select one of the languages in the South for use, together with Arabic, as the main vehicle of communication among uneducated people. The teaching of this same Southern language in schools of the North would be of great value. The study and use of the minority language groups by the majority language groups promotes integration. A Northerner communicating with a Dinka in the latter's language will, no doubt, inspire confidence and a sense of equality,[32] which would encourage mutual understanding. Dinka might prove to be the language which can contribute to this objective. The promotion of Arabic in the South as a means of communication remains, however, the main instrument in this direction.

Religion, like language, has been an area of conflict. The conflict has sometimes been presented as being between Christianity and Islam, the assumption being that all the Southerners are Christians, but this is not true. The Commission of Enquiry in 1955 estimated that in the South there were about 40,500 Muslims and 230,000 Christians; the number of those committed to one indigenous faith or another was estimated at 3,000,000 or about 90 per cent of the population. Recently church sources have claimed that there are about 500,000 to 600,000 Christians in the South,[33] which means that of the population today more than 90 per cent are non-Christian. On the other hand, not only Christians and non-Muslims were involved in the conflict; although very few, some Muslims took part in the rebellion.

The roots of the conflict cannot, therefore, be described as religious. Religion has been used to promote the conflict. As long ago as 1892 and before the Sudan was reconquered, Kitchener wrote as follows:

'Unless the Christian powers hold their own in Africa, the Mohammedan Arabs will, I believe, step in and in the centre of the continent form a base from which they will be able to drive back all civilizing influences to the coast, and the country will then be given up to slavery and misrule, as is the case in the Sudan at present.'[34] This warning about Islam shaped the religious policy followed by the Condominium administration. Christian missionary societies were encouraged while Islam was discouraged. This became part and parcel of the Southern policy. Christianity thus became associated in the minds of educated Northerners with the policy of separation.

It was natural therefore for the different governments in the North after independence to try and reverse the old policy and promote Islam with a view to promoting political integration and solving the Southern problem. 'This policy', writes Othwan Dak, 'was no doubt intended to promote a political re-orientation and inculcation of national consciousness among Southern Sudanese.'[35] Those who were made responsible for applying the policy were not always concerned with religion as a factor of political integration. They were concerned with Islam as a religion and less with its political and social aspects. This was resisted in the South and outside the Sudan by the missionaries. It was claimed by them that Christianity was being suppressed and persecuted in the Southern Sudan in favour of Islam.

Freedom of religious opinion, and the right to profess it publicly and privately and to establish religious institutions, has been recognized in the Addis Ababa Agreement. Later, Article 16 of the Sudan's Constitution recognizes both Islam and Christianity as religions of the state. Other beliefs referred to as 'noble spiritual beliefs'[36] are also recognized but not on the same level as Christianity and Islam. In Article 9 of the Constitution, both Islamic law and custom are recognized as the main sources of legislation. The more important aspect of the Constitution is not however the recognition given in it to Islam, Christianity and other beliefs; it is the refusal, after long and heated debates, to describe the Sudan as an Islamic republic. Another important aspect of the Constitution is its rejection of the exploitation of religion for political ends. According to Article 16 of the Constitution, 'any act which is intended or is likely to promote feelings of hatred, enmity or discord among religious communities shall be contrary to the Constitution and punishable by law.'[3][7]

Constitutions and laws are one thing and implementation and practice are another. Religion can be both an integrating and a disintegrating factor, depending on those who administer religious instruction. During the Condominium administration, the European missionaries were closely associated with the colonial power and used the religious issue to promote separation. After independence the European missionary organizations participated more in the promotion of conflict than in the promotion of peace. It was only when the All Africa Conference of Churches became involved and the World Council of Churches set out to find the truth about the problem and freed itself of the old concepts, that the religious issue was put in the right perspective.

In the Northern Sudan too, there are still those who believe that integration can only come through Islamization. It is true that the existence of one religion facilitates integration, but religion is not the only and decisive factor. Although the West African settlers in the Sudan profess Islam, their integration into Sudanese society has not yet been complete.

Confrontation in the past was, therefore, not between Islam and Christianity as such but between the foreign missionary organizations and the governments in the North which are predominantly Muslim. The religious freedoms guaranteed in the Constitution are for Sudanese and not for foreign agencies. The Sudan, according to the Constitution, is a secular state. The promotion of these concepts and their acceptance and practice would reduce the chance of religion becoming a source of conflict.

In addition to this, the encouragement of contact between the Southerners and Northerners will promote mutual knowledge and better understanding. In the past, few Southerners travelled to the North, and this contributed to lack of knowledge and misunderstanding. Migration to the North has, however, increased in recent years. Southerners go North to seek employment in the urban areas – especially Khartoum, Omdurman and Khartoum North – and in the Gezira. Farnham Rehfisch writes as follows: 'In the past, few Southerners ventured North, largely because the Condominium government followed the policy of attempting to isolate the North from the South and did their best to prohibit population movement from one region to the other. In the last decade this policy was abandoned and there has been a large exodus from the South to the North.'[38] Once they are in the Northern towns, the Southerners try to integrate. They try to speak Arabic and adopt the habits of the Northern Sudanese. They may not always immediately succeed in achieving social integration, but the contacts they make lay the foundations for better knowledge and understanding.

Another aspect of contact is through common employment, especially in factories and government offices. Common conditions of work stimulate common actions and reactions and promote a sense of unity and tolerance. Peter McLoughlin writes of Omdurman as follows: 'The continuous contact of diverse religious and nationality groups in both employment and society has resulted in a sophisticated and active spirit of tolerance and progress, perhaps unmatched on the African continent.'[39] The urban centres are usually places where a spirit of tolerance prevails. This characteristic of urban centres makes them attractive to migrants seeking employment and they have a greater potential for promoting integration than the less urbanized areas. It may take some time before mistrust and misunderstanding are completely overcome, yet the integrative behaviour generated will contribute towards the development of a national identity.

Action in these areas, however, needs to be supplemented by action on other fronts: those of administration, ideology and foreign relations. The existence of effective government at national and regional levels is a pre-requisite for the development and promotion of national unity.

Party politics, party divisions and ideological confusion have contributed in the past to the instability and ineffectiveness of Sudanese government and have promoted dissent and conflict, not only between the North and the South, but also within each region. The Sudan's new Constitution rejects the multi-party system of government, establishing in its place the Sudanese Socialist Union as the sole political organization in the country.[40] Socialism, where 'the State shall own and manage the fundamental means of production in the economy',[41] replaces the various ideologies of the past.

It has been suggested that unlike 'the 9th of June, 1969, declaration which has put great emphasis on the building of a socialist democratic movement in the South, linked to the socialist movement in the North',[42] the Southern Provinces Self-Government Act 1972 has failed to mention this important requirement. This is true in the sense that the building of a democratic socialist movement has not been made a pre-requisite for the achievement of regional self-government. It is not, however, true in another sense. The 9th of June declaration is entrenched in the Agreement, and regional self-government is conceived within a united socialist Sudan.

It has also been suggested that regional self-government for the South with its concepts of decentralization will encourage 'other regions in the country which have distinguished ethnic and socio-cultural identities to have similar political and administrative arrangements'.[43] It is asked whether it is not possible that the Nuba Mountains region, Darfur, Kordofan, the Beja area and the Fung region, which have many characteristics that differentiate them from the areas adjacent to them, 'already showing regional tendencies and seeing the South granted regional self-government, would demand equal political and administrative arrangements.'[44] The comparison between these regions and the South is invalid. In none of them did a military secessionist movement arise. They did not experience the same strained relations with the central government as the South. Geographically and historically they are part of the North; none of them has the characteristics and background of the South, which rightly justify the latter's constitution as a self-governing region within the Sudan.

As to foreign policy, the realization that Pan-Africanism and Pan-Arabism are not necessarily exclusive and that the Sudan is at the centre of Africa and at the same time part of the Arab World, is the first step towards constructing a foreign policy that would contribute to this end. This was not the case before 1969. Then the Sudan emphasized its relations with its neighbours to the North to the exclusion of its neighbours to the East, South and West, relations with whom were often strained – due largely to the Southern problem. The conflict in the Middle East and Israeli activities in the Southern Sudan and in neighbouring African countries contributed to this situation.

The solution of the Southern problem, the containment of Israeli activities in Africa, and the active involvement of the Sudan in the activities of the O.A.U. will enable the Sudan to promote friendly relations with all its neighbours. The Sudan, which has borders with eight countries, and with its ethnic and cultural composition, cannot afford to develop a one-sided foreign policy. A national and balanced policy that takes into consideration these facts will contribute to the promotion of national unity.

This, however, will require active participation of the regional government in the making of foreign policy. According to the Addis Ababa Agreement, the regional government has no powers in external affairs; but this should not be interpreted so as to exclude participation by the South in the decision-making process and in the execution of the policy itself.

Finally, the processes of integrating groups that are culturally and socially different from each other into a single territorial unit, and of establishing national identity – nation-building – are long ones. It does not happen overnight, nor does it happen through political and administrative decisions alone. The process must be designed and the programme of action planned and seen to be executed. This plan will require the collection of information and studies on the different aspects of life in the South. Many changes have taken place in the last twenty years, and most of the little information we have has been contributed by outsiders. The interests of the Sudan and of the South were not always the main motivation. The need for research and studies by economists, anthropologists, political scientists, historians, geographers and others is obvious. It is towards this end, and towards the establishment of permanent peace and unity in the Sudan, that all efforts and action, should be directed.

REFERENCES

1. Ali Mazrui. The comment was made at a conference on development strategies in Africa in 1970, held by the University of Dar es Salaam in Arusha, 17–22 September, 1973.

2. J. Bowyer Bell, 'The Sudan's African Policy: Problems and Prospects', *Africa Today*, Vol. 20, No. 3 (Summer 1973).

3. Oliver Albino, *op. cit.*, p. VI.

4. *Ibid.*

5. Bell, *op. cit.*

6. For a discussion of this see Muddathir Abdel Rahim, *Arabism, Africanism and Self-identification in the Sudan*; Ali Mazrui, 'The Multiple Marginality of the Sudan', in Yusuf Fadl Hassan (ed.), *Sudan in Africa*, Khartoum, 1971, and O. Aguda, 'Arabism and Pan-Arabism in Sudanese Politics', *Journal of Modern African Studies*, June 1973, pp. 177–200.

7. O. Aguda, *op. cit.*, p. 183.

8. Zeine M. Zein, *The Emergence of Arab Nationalism*, Beirut 1966.

9. *Ibid.*

10. Ali Mazrui, *op. cit.*, p. 242.

11. *Ibid.*, p. 240.

12. Muddathir Abdel Rahim, *op. cit.*, p. 228.

13. Ali Mazrui, *op. cit.*, p. 254.

14. The Democratic Republic of the Sudan, *Permanent Constitution of the Sudan*, Khartoum, May 1973, p. 2.

15. *Ibid.*, p. 3.

16. *Ibid.*, p. 4.

17. *Ibid.*

18. Rafia Hassan Ahmed, 'The Prospects of Regional Government in the Sudan with special reference to the South', M.Sc. thesis, University of Khartoum, April 1973, p. 156.

19. *Ibid.*, p. 167.

20. *Ibid.*

21. Rudolph Ibrahim Samuel, 'Economic Structure of the Southern Sudan', Fifth Erkawit Conference, Juba, January 1971.

22. John Wallis Sommer, 'The Sudan: a Geographical Investigation of the Historical and Social Roots of Political Dissension', Ph.D. thesis Boston University, 1958, p. 195.

23. R. I. Samuel, *op. cit.*

24. Godfrey Lienhardt, *The Western Dinka*, quoted in Sommer, *op. cit.*, p. 198.

25. Sommer, *op. cit.*, pp. 199–200.

26. *Ibid.*, p. 202.

27. Othwan Dak, 'Southern Sudan: the Primacy of Socio-economic Development', Fifth Erkawit Conference, Juba, 1971, p. 4.

28. The Addis Ababa Agreement, Chapters IV and VIII, Appendix 7.

29. H. A. Morrice, 'The Development of Sudan's Communications', *Sudan Notes and Records*, XXX, 1949.

30. Wilfred Owen, *Strategy for Mobility*, Brookings Institution: Washington D.C., 1964.

31. The Addis Ababa Agreement, Appendix 7.

32. Sommer, *op. cit.*, p. 238.

33. *East Africa Reporter*, August 17, 1963, quoted in Sommer, *op. cit.*, p. 109.

34. Kitchener's Memorandum on Uganda, September 1892, quoted in Sommer, *op. cit.*, p. 215.

35. Othwan Dak, *op. cit.*, p. 5.

36. Democratic Republic of the Sudan, *Permanent Constitution*, Khartoum, May 1973, p. 4.

37. *Ibid.*, p. 4.

38. F. Rehfisch, 'A Study of some Southern Migrants in Omdurman', *Sudan Notes and Records*, XLIII, 1962.

39. P. McLoughlin, 'The Sudan's Three Towns', *Economic Development and Cultural Change*, XII No. 3, April 1964, pp. 286–304.

40. Sudan's Constitution, p. 2.

41. *Ibid.*

42. Rafia Hassan Ahmed, *op. cit.*, p. 187.

43. *Ibid.*, p. 198.

44. *Ibid.*, p. 199.

POLICY STATEMENT ON THE SOUTHERN QUESTION BY PRESIDENT NIMEIRI, 9 JUNE 1969

Dear Countrymen! Warm congratulations and greetings to you on this historic occasion of your revolution.

No doubt you have heard of the broad aims of the revolution outlined in my speech and in that of the Prime Minister which was broadcast on 25 May. Our revolution is the continuation of the October 21 popular revolution. It works for the regeneration of life in our country, for social progress and the raising of the standard of living of the masses of our people throughout the country. It stands against imperialism, colonialism and whole-heartedly supports the liberation movements of the African and Arab peoples as well as other peoples throughout the world.

A Historical Background

Dear Countrymen, the Revolutionary Government is fully aware of the magnitude of the Southern problem and is determined to arrive at a lasting solution.

This problem has deep-going historical roots dating back to the last century. It is the result of the policies of British Colonialism which left the legacy of uneven development between the Northern and Southern parts of the country, with the result that on the advent of independence Southerners found themselves in an unequal position with their Northern brethren in every field.

The traditional circles and parties that have held the reins of power in our country since independence have utterly failed to solve the Southern question. They have exploited state power for self-enrichment and for serving narrow partisan interests without caring about the interests of the masses of our people whether in the North or in the South.

It is important to realise also that most of the Southern leaders contributed a great deal to the present deterioration of the state of affairs in that part of our beloved country. Over the years, since 1950 to the present day they have sought alliances with the Northern reactionary circles and with imperialism whether from inside or outside the borders. Personal gain was the mainspring of their actions.

Dear Countrymen, the enemies of the North are also the enemies of the South. The common enemy is imperialism and neo-colonialism, which is oppressing and exploiting the African and Arab peoples, and standing in the way of their advance. Internally, our common enemies are the reactionary forces of counter-revolution. The 25 May Revolution is not the same as the *coup d'état* of November 1958. That was a reactionary move staged by the imperialists in alliance with local reaction in and outside the army. It was made to silence the demands of the masses of our people both in the North and the South for social change and genuine democracy.

The Revolution of May 25 is the very opposite of the *coup d'état* of 1958. Our revolution is, we repeat, directed against imperialism, the reactionary circles and corrupt parties that destroyed the October Revolution and were aiming at finally liquidating any progressive movement and installing a reactionary dictatorship.

Dear Countrymen, the revolutionary Government is confident and competent enough to face existing realities. It recognises the historical and cultural differences between the North and South and firmly believes that the unity of our country must be built upon these objective realities. The Southern people have the right to develop their respective cultures and traditions within a united Socialist Sudan.

In furtherance of these objectives the Revolutionary Council and the Council of Ministers held joint meetings and after a full discussion of the matter resolved to recognise the right of the Southern people to Regional Autonomy within a united Sudan.

Regional Autonomy Programme

You will realise that the building of a broad socialist-oriented democratic movement in the South, forming part of the revolutionary structure in the North and capable of assuming the reins of power in that region and rebuffing imperialist penetration and infiltration from the rear, is an essential pre-requisite for the practical and healthy application of Regional Autonomy.

Within this framework and in order to prepare for that day when this right can be exercised, the Revolutionary Government is drawing up the following programme:

1. the continuation and further extension of the Amnesty Law;
2. economic, social and cultural development of the South;
3. the appointment of a Minister for Southern Affairs;
4. the training of personnel.

The Government will create a special economic planning board for the South and will prepare a special budget for the South, which aims at the development of the Southern provinces at the shortest possible time.

Dear Southern Countrymen, in order that we may be able to carry out this programme it is of the utmost importance that peace and security should prevail in the South and that life return to normal. It is primarily the responsibility of you all whether you be in the bush or at home to maintain peace and stability. The way is open for those abroad to return home and co-operate with us in building a prosperous Sudan, united and democratic.

THE ADDIS ABABA AGREEMENT ON THE PROBLEM OF SOUTH SUDAN

*Draft Organic Law to organize Regional
Self-Government in the Southern Provinces of
the Democratic Republic of the Sudan*

In accordance with the provisions of the Constitution of the Democratic Republic of the Sudan and in realization of the memorable May Revolution Declaration of June 9, 1969, granting the Southern Provinces of the Sudan Regional Self-Government within a united socialist Sudan, and in accordance with the principle of the May Revolution that the Sudanese people participate actively in and supervise the decentralized system of the government of their country, it is hereunder enacted:

Article 1. This law shall be called the law for Regional Self-Government in the Southern Provinces. It shall come into force on a date within a period not exceeding thirty days from the date of the Addis Ababa Agreement.

Article 2. This law shall be issued as an organic law which cannot be amended except by a three-quarters majority of the People's National Assembly and confirmed by a two-thirds majority in a referendum held in the three Southern Provinces of the Sudan.

CHAPTER II: DEFINITIONS

Article 3.
   (i) 'Constitution' refers to the Republican Order No. 5 or any other basic law replacing or amending it.

(ii) 'President' means the President of the Democratic Republic of the Sudan.

(iii) 'Southern Provinces of the Sudan' means the Provinces of Bahr El Ghazal, Equatoria and Upper Nile in accordance with their boundaries as they stood on January 1, 1956, and any other areas that were culturally and geographically a part of the Southern Complex as may be decided by a referendum.

(iv) 'People's Regional Assembly' refers to the legislative body for the Southern Region of the Sudan.

(v) 'High Executive Council' refers to the Executive Council appointed by the President on the recommendation of the President of the High Executive Council and such body shall supervise the administration and direct public affairs in the Southern Region of the Sudan.

(vi) 'President of the High Executive Council' refers to the person appointed by the President on the recommendation of the People's Regional Assembly to lead and supervise the executive organs responsible for the administration of the Southern Provinces.

(vii) 'People's National Assembly' refers to the National Legislative Assembly representing the people of the Sudan in accordance with the constitution.

(viii) 'Sudanese' refers to any Sudanese citizen as defined by the Sudanese Nationality Act 1957 and any amendments thereof.

CHAPTER III

Article 4. The Provinces of Bahr El Ghazal, Equatoria and Upper Nile as defined in Article 3 (iii) shall constitute a self-governing Region within the Democratic Republic of the Sudan and shall be known as the Southern Region.

Article 5. The Southern Region shall have legislative and executive organs, the functions and powers of which are defined by this law.

Article 6. Arabic shall be the official language for the Sudan and English the principal language for the Southern Region

without prejudice to the use of any other language or
languages which may serve a practical necessity for the
efficient and expeditious discharge of executive and administrative functions of the Region.

CHAPTER IV

Article 7. Neither the People's Regional Assembly nor the
High Executive Council shall legislate or exercise any powers
on matters of national nature which are:

   (i) National Defence
  (ii) External Affairs
 (iii) Currency and Coinage
  (iv) Air and Inter-Regional River Transport
   (v) Communications and Telecommunications
  (vi) Customs and Foreign Trade except for border trade
        and certain commodities which the Regional Govern-
        ment may specify with the approval of the Central
        Government.
 (vii) Nationality and Immigration (Emigration)
(viii) Planning for Economic and Social Development
  (ix) Educational Planning
   (x) Public-Audit.

CHAPTER V: LEGISLATURE

Article 8. Regional Legislation in the Southern Region is
exercised by a People's Regional Assembly elected by
Sudanese Citizens resident in the Southern Region. The
constitution and conditions of membership of the Assembly
shall be determined by law.

Article 9. Members of the People's Regional Assembly shall
be elected by direct secret ballot.

Article 10.
   (i) For the First Assembly the President may appoint
        additional members to the People's Regional Assem-
        bly where conditions for elections are not conducive
        to such elections as stipulated in Article 9, provided

      that such appointed members shall not exceed one-quarter of the Assembly.

(ii) The People's Regional Assembly shall regulate the conduct of its business in accordance with rules of procedures to be laid down by the said Assembly during its first sitting.

(iii) The People's Regional Assembly shall elect one of its members as a speaker, provided that the first sitting shall be presided over by the Interim President of the High Executive Council.

Article 11. The People's Regional Assembly shall legislate for the preservation of public order, internal security, efficient administration and the development of the Southern Region in cultural, economic and social fields and in particular in the following:—

(i) Promotion and utilization of Regional financial resources for the development and administration of the Southern Region.

(ii) Organization of the machinery for Regional and Local Administration.

(iii) Legislation on traditional law and custom within the framework of National Law.

(iv) Establishment, maintenance and administration of prisons and reformatory institutions.

(v) Establishment, maintenance and administration of Public Schools at all levels in accordance with National Plans for education and economic and social development.

(vi) Promotion of local languages and cultures.

(vii) Town and village planning and the construction of roads in accordance with National Plans and programmes.

(viii) Promotion of trade; establishment of local industries and markets; issue of traders' licences and formation of co-operative societies.

(ix) Establishment, maintenance and administration of public hospitals.

(x) Administration of environmental health services; maternity care; child welfare; supervision of markets;

combat of epidemic diseases; training of medical assistants and rural midwives; establishment of health centres, dispensaries and dressing stations.

(xi)   Promotion of animal health; control of epidemics and improvement of animal production and trade.

(xii) Promotion of tourism.

(xiii) Establishment of zoological gardens, museums, organizations of trade and cultural exhibitions.

(xiv) Mining and quarrying without prejudice to the right of the Central Government in the event of the discovery of natural gas and minerals.

(xv)   Recruitment for, organization and administration of Police and Prison services in accordance with the national policy and standards.

(xvi) Land use in accordance with national laws and plans.

(xvii) Control and prevention of pests and plant diseases.

(xviii) Development, utilization, and protection of forests, crops and pastures in accordance with national laws.

(xix) Promotion and encouragement of self-help programmes.

(xx)   All other matters delegated by the President or the People's National Assembly for legislation.

Article 12. The People's National Assembly may call for facts and information concerning the conduct of administration in the Southern Region.

Article 13.

(i)   The People's Regional Assembly may, by a three-quarters majority and for specified reasons relating to public interest, request the President to relieve the President or any member of the High Executive Council from office. The President shall accede to such request.

(ii) In case of vacancy, relief or resignation of the President of the High Executive Council, the entire body shall be considered as having automatically resigned.

Article 14. The People's Regional Assembly may, by a two-thirds majority, request the President to postpone the coming into force of any law which, in the view of the members, adversely affects the welfare and interests of the citizens of the Southern Region. The President may, if he thinks fit, accede to such request.

Article 15.
  (i)   The People's Regional Assembly may, by a majority of its members, request the President to withdraw any Bill presented to the People's National Assembly which in their view affects adversely the welfare, rights or interests of the citizens in the Southern Region, pending communication of the views of the People's Regional Assembly.
  (ii) If the President accedes to such request, the People's Regional Assembly shall present its views within 15 days from the date of accession to the request.
  (iii) The President shall communicate any such views to the People's National Assembly together with his own observations if he deems necessary.

Article 16. The People's National Assembly shall communicate all Bills and Acts to the People's Regional Assembly for their information. The People's Regional Assembly shall act similarly.

CHAPTER VI: THE EXECUTIVE

Article 17. The Regional Executive Authority is vested in a High Executive Council which acts on behalf of the President.

Article 18. The High Executive Council shall specify the duties of the various departments in the Southern Region provided that on matters relating to Central Government Agencies it shall act with the approval of the President.

Article 19. The President of the High Executive Council shall be appointed and relieved of office by the President on the recommendation of the People's Regional Assembly.

Article 20. The High Executive Council shall be composed of members appointed and relieved of office by the President on the recommendation of the President of the High Executive Council.

Article 21. The President of the High Executive Council and its members are responsible to the President and to the People's Regional Assembly for efficient administration in the Southern Region. They shall take an oath of office before the President.

Article 22. The President and members of the High Executive Council may attend meetings of the People's Regional Assembly and participate in its deliberations without the right to vote, unless they are also members of the People's Regional Assembly.

CHAPTER VII

Article 23. The President shall from time to time regulate the relationship between the High Executive Council and the central ministries.

Article 24. The High Executive Council may initiate laws for the creation of a Regional Public Service. These laws shall specify the terms and conditions of service for the Regional Public Service.

CHAPTER VIII: FINANCE

Article 25. The People's Regional Assembly may levy Regional duties and taxes in addition to National and Local duties and taxes. It may issue legislation and orders to guarantee the collection of all public monies at different levels.

(*a*) The source of revenue of the Southern Region shall consist of the following: —
  (i) Direct and indirect regional taxes.
  (ii) Contributions from People's Local Government Councils.
  (iii) Revenue from commercial, industrial and agricultural projects in the Region in accordance with the National Plan.

(iv) Funds from the National Treasury for established services.

(v) Funds voted by the People's National Assembly in accordance with the requirements of the Region.

(vi) The Special Development Budget for the South as presented by the People's Regional Assembly for the acceleration of economic and social advancement of the Southern Region as envisaged in the declaration of June 9, 1968.

(vii) See Appendix B.

(viii) Any other sources.

(*b*) The Regional Executive Council shall prepare a budget to meet the expenditure of regional services, security, administration, and development in accordance with national plans and programmes and shall submit it to the People's Regional Assembly for approval.

CHAPTER IX: OTHER PROVISIONS

Article 27.

(i) Citizens of the Southern Region shall constitute a sizeable proportion of the People's Armed Forces in such reasonable numbers as will correspond to the population of the region.

(ii) The use of the People's Armed Forces within the Region and outside the framework of national defence shall be controlled by the President on the advice of the President of the High Executive Council.

(iii) Temporary arrangements for the composition of units of the People's Armed Forces in the Southern Region are provided for in the Protocol on Interim Arrangements.

Article 28. The President may veto any Bill which he deems contrary to the Provisions of the National Constitution provided the People's Regional Assembly, after receiving the President's views, may reintroduce the Bill.

Article 29. The President and members of the High Executive Council may initiate laws in the People's Regional Assembly.

Article 30. Any member of the People's Regional Assembly may initiate any law provided that financial Bills shall not be presented without sufficient notice to the President of the High Executive Council.

Article 31. The People's Regional Assembly shall strive to consolidate the unity of the Sudan and respect the spirit of the National Constitution.

Article 32. All citizens are guaranteed freedom of movement in and out of the Southern Region, provided restriction or prohibition of movement may be imposed on a named citizen or citizens solely on grounds of public health and order.

Article 33.
    (i) All citizens resident in the Southern Region are guaranteed equal opportunity of education, employment, commerce and the practice of any profession.
   (ii) No law may adversely affect the rights of citizens enumerated in the previous item on the basis of race, tribal origin, religion, place of birth, or sex.

Article 34. Juba shall be the Capital of the Southern Region and the seat of the Regional Executive and Legislature.

APPENDIX A: FUNDAMENTAL RIGHTS AND FREEDOMS

The following should be guaranteed by the Constitution of the Democratic Republic of the Sudan.
1. A citizen should not be deprived of his citizenship.
2. Equality of citizens.
    (i) All citizens, without distinction based on race, national origin, birth, language, sex, economic or social status, should have equal rights and duties before the law.
   (ii) All persons should be equal before the courts of law and should have the right to institute legal proceedings in order to remove any injustice or declare any right in an open court without delay prejudicing their interests.

3. Personal liberty.
   (i) Penal liability should be personal. Any kind of collective punishment should be prohibited.
   (ii) The accused should be presumed innocent until proved guilty.
   (iii) Retrospective penal legislation and punishment should be prohibited.
   (iv) The right of the accused to defend himself personally or through an agent should be guaranteed.
   (v) No person should be arrested, detained or imprisoned except in accordance with the due process of law, and no person should remain in custody or detention for more than twenty-four hours without judicial order.
   (vi) No accused person should be subjected to inducement, intimidation or torture in order to extract evidence from him whether in his favour or against him or against any other person, and no humiliating punishment should be inflicted on any convicted person.
4. Freedom of Religion and Conscience.
   (i) Every person should enjoy freedom of religious opinion and of conscience and the right to profess them publicly and privately and to establish religious institutions subject to reasonable limitations in favour of morality, health or public order as prescribed by law.
   (ii) Parents and guardians should be guaranteed the right to educate their children and those under their care in accordance with the relation of their choice.
5. Protection of labour.
   (i) Forced and compulsory labour of any kind should be prohibited except when ordered for military or civil necessity or pursuant to penal punishment prescribed by law.
   (ii) The right to equal pay for equal work should be guaranteed.
6. Freedom of minority to use their languages and develop their culture should be guaranteed.

APPENDIX B: DRAFT ORDINANCE ON ITEMS OF REVENUE AND
GRANTS-IN-AID FOR THE SOUTHERN REGION

1. Profits accruing to the Central Government as a result of exporting products of the Southern Region.
2. Business Profit Tax of the Southern Region that are at present in the central list of the Ministry of Treasury.
3. Excise Duties on alcoholic beverages and spirits consumed in the Southern Region.
4. Profits on sugar consumed in the Southern Region.
5. Royalties on forest products of the Southern Region.
6. Royalties on leaf Tobacco and Cigarettes.
7. Taxation on property other than that provided in the Rates Ordinance.
8. Taxes and Rates on Central and Local Government Projects (5 per cent of net profits of factories, co-operative societies, agricultural enterprises and cinemas).
9. Revenue accruing from Central Government activities in the Southern Region provided the Region shall bear maintenance expenses e.g., Post Office revenue, land sales, sale of forms and documents, stamp duties and any other item to be specified from time to time.
10. Licences other than those provided for in the People's Local Government Act, 1971.
11. Special Development Tax to be paid by Residents in the Southern Region the rate of which should be decided by the People's Regional Assembly.
12. Income Tax collected from officials and employees serving in the Southern Region both in the local and national civil services as well as in the Army, Police and Prisons, Judiciary, and Political Establishment.
13. Corporation Tax on any factory and/or agricultural project established in the Region but not run by the Regional Government (5 per cent of the initial cost).
14. Contributions from the Central Government for the encouragement of construction and development; for every agricultural project, industrial project and trading enterprise (20 per cent of the initial cost as assessed by the Central Government).
15. New Social Service Projects to be established by the

Region or any of its Local Government units, and for which funds are allocated, shall receive grants from the National Treasury in the following manner:

Education institutions, 20 per cent of expenses

Trunk and through Roads and Bridges, 25 per cent of expenses

Relief and Social amenities, 15 per cent of expenses

. Tourist attraction projects, 25 per cent of expenses

Security, 15 per cent of expenses

Grants for Post Secondary and University education within the Sudan, 20 per cent of grants, outside the Sudan 30 per cent of grants

Contribution for Research, Scientific Advancement, and Cultural Activities, 25 per cent of expenses.

AGREEMENT ON THE CEASE-FIRE IN THE SOUTHERN REGION

Article 1. This Agreement shall come into force on the date and time specified for the ratification of the Addis Ababa Agreement.

Article 2. There will be an end to all military operations and to all armed actions in the Southern Region from the time of cease-fire.

Article 3. All combat forces shall remain in the area under their control at the time of the cease-fire.

Article 4. Both parties agree to forbid any individual or collective acts of violence.

Any underground activities contrary to public order shall cease.

Article 5. Movements of individual members of both combat forces outside the areas under their control shall be allowed only if these individuals are unarmed and authorized by their respective authorities. The plans for stationing troops from the National Army shall be such as to avoid any contact between them and the Southern Sudan Liberation Movement combat forces.

Article 6. A Joint Commission is hereby created for the implementation of all questions related to the cease-fire including repatriation of refugees. The Joint Commission shall include members from all the countries bordering on the Southern Region as well as representatives of the International Committee of the Red Cross, World Council of Churches, All Africa Conference of Churches and United Nations High Commissioner for Refugees.

Article 7. The Joint Commission shall propose all measures to be undertaken by both parties in dealing with all incidents after a full inquiry on the spot.

Article 8. Each party shall be represented on the Joint Commission by one senior military officer and a maximum of five other members.

Article 9. The headquarters of the Joint Commission shall be located in Juba with provincial branches in Juba, Malakal and Wau.

Article 10. The Joint Commission shall appoint local commissions in various centres of the Southern Region composed of two members from each party.

PROTOCOLS ON INTERIM ARRANGEMENTS

CHAPTER I: INTERIM ADMINISTRATIVE ARRANGEMENTS

(*Political, Local Government and Civil Service*)

Article 1. The President of the Democratic Republic of the Sudan shall, in consultation with the Southern Sudan Liberation Movement (S.S.L.M.) and branches of the Sudanese Socialist Union in the Southern Region, appoint the President and members of an Interim High Executive Council.

Article 2. The Interim High Executive Council shall consist of the President and other members with portfolios in:

(*a*) Finance and Economic Planning.
(*b*) Education.
(*c*) Information, Culture and Tourism.
(*d*) Communication and Transport.
(*e*) Agriculture, Animal Production and Fisheries.
(*f*) Public Health.
(*g*) Regional Administration (Local Government, Legal Affairs, Police and Prisons).
(*h*) Housing, Public Works and Utilities.
(*i*) Natural Resources and Rural Development (Land Use, Rural Water Supply, Forestry and Co-operatives).
(*j*) Public Service and Labour.
(*k*) Minerals and Industry, Trade and Supply.

Article 3. The Interim High Executive Council shall, in accordance with national laws, establish a Regional Civil Service subject to ratification by the People's Regional Assembly.

Article 4. The President shall, in consultation with the Interim High Executive Council, determine the date for the election to the People's Regional Assembly, and the Interim High Executive Council shall make arrangements for the setting up of this Assembly.

Article 5. In order to facilitate the placement in and appointment to both central and regional institutions, the Southern Sudan Liberation Movement shall compile and communicate lists of citizens of the Southern Region outside the Sudan in accordance with details to be supplied by the Ministry of Public Service and Administrative Reform.

Article 6. The Interim High Executive Council and the Ministry of Public Service and Administrative Reform shall undertake to provide necessary financial allocations with effect from the 1972–73 Budget for such placements and appointments.

Article 7. The Mandate of the Interim High Executive Council shall not exceed a period of 18 months.

CHAPTER II: TEMPORARY ARRANGEMENTS FOR THE
COMPOSITION OF UNITS OF THE PEOPLE'S ARMED FORCES IN
THE SOUTHERN REGION

Article 1. These arrangements shall remain in force for a
period of five years subject to revision by the President on
the request of the President of the High Executive Council
acting with the consent of the People's Regional Assembly.

Article 2. The People's Armed Forces in the Southern Region
shall consist of a national force called the Southern Command composed of 12,000 officers and men of whom 6,000
shall be citizens from the Region and the other 6,000 from
outside the Region.

Article 3. The recruitment and integration of citizens from
the Southern Region within the aforementioned Forces shall
be determined by a Joint Military Commission taking into
account the need for initial separate deployment of troops
with a view to achieve smooth integration in the national
force. The Commission shall ensure that this deployment
shall be such that an atmosphere of peace and confidence
shall prevail in the Southern Region.

Article 4. The Joint Military Commission shall be composed
of three senior military officers from each side. Decisions of
the Joint Military Commission shall be taken unanimously. In
case of disagreement such matters shall be referred to the
respective authorities.

CHAPTER III: AMNESTY AND JUDICIAL ARRANGEMENTS

Article 1. No action or other legal proceedings whatsoever,
civil or criminal, shall be instituted against any person in any
court of law for or on account of any act or matter done
inside or outside the Sudan as from the 18th day of August
1955, if such act or matter was done in connection with
mutiny, rebellion or sedition in the Southern Region.

Article 2. If a civil suit in relation to any acts or matters
referred to in Article 1 is instituted before or after the date
of ratification of the Addis Ababa Agreement such a suit
shall be discharged and made null and void.

Article 3. All persons serving terms of imprisonment or held in detention in respect of offences herein before specified in Article 1 shall be discharged or released within 15 days from the date of ratification of the Addis Ababa Agreement.

Article 4. The Joint Cease-Fire Commission shall keep a register of all civilian returnees, which register shall serve to certify that the persons therein named are considered indemnified within the meaning of this Agreement provided that the Commission may delegate such power to the Diplomatic Missions of the Democratic Republic of the Sudan in the case of citizens from the Southern Region living abroad and to whom the provisions of this Agreement apply.

Article 5. In the case of armed returnees or those belonging to combat forces the Joint Military Commission shall keep a similar register of those persons who shall be treated in the same manner as provided for in Article 4.

Article 6. Notwithstanding the provisions of Articles 4 and 5 above a Special Tribunal with ad hoc judicial powers shall be established to examine and decide on those cases which in the estimation of the authorities do not meet the conditions for amnesty specified in Article 1 of this Agreement. The Special Tribunal shall be composed of a President appointed by the President of the Republic and not more than four members named by the Cease-Fire Commission.

Article 7. Cases referred to in Article 6 shall be brought to the attention of the Special Tribunal by request of the Minister of Justice.

Article 8. The Amnesty Provisions contained in this Agreement as well as the powers of the Special Tribunal shall remain in force until such time as the President after consultation with the commissions referred to in this Agreement, decide that they have fulfilled their functions.

CHAPTER IV:
REPATRIATION AND RESETTLEMENT COMMISSION

1. *Repatriation*

Article 1. There shall be established a Special|Commission inside and where required outside the Southern Region charged with the responsibility of taking all administrative and other measures as may be necessary in order to repatriate all citizens from the Southern Region who today are residing in other countries and especially in the neighbouring countries.

The headquarters of the Commission shall be in Juba.

Article 2. The Commission shall be composed of at least three members including one representative of the Central Government, one representative of the Southern Region and one representative of the U.N. High Commissioner for Refugees. For those commissions operating outside the Sudan, a representative of the host Government shall be included, plus the Central Government representative who shall be the Ambassador of the Sudan or his representative.

Article 3. The control of repatriation at the borders shall be assumed by the competent border authorities in co-operation with the representatives of the Resettlement Commission.

Article 4. The repatriation commission shall work very closely with the Commission for Relief and Resettlement to ensure that the operation and timing of the returning of refugees from across the borders is adequately co-ordinated.

II. *Resettlement*

Article 1. There shall be established a Special Commission for Relief and Resettlement under the President of the Interim High Executive Council with headquarters in Juba and provincial branches in Juba, Malakal and Wau. The Commission, its branches and whatever units it may deem fit to create in other localities in order to facilitate its functions, shall be responsible for co-ordination and implementation of all relief services and planning related to Resettlement and Rehabilitation of all returnees, that is:

    (*a*) Refugees from neighbouring countries;
    (*b*) Displaced persons resident in the main centres of the Southern Region and other parts of the Sudan;
    (*c*) Displaced persons including residual Anya Nya personnel and supporters in the bush;
    (*d*) Handicapped and orphans.

Article 2. Although resettlement and rehabilitation of refugees and displaced persons is administratively the responsibility of the Regional Government the present conditions in the Southern Region dictate that efforts of the whole nation of the Sudan and International Organizations should be pooled to help and rehabilitate persons affected by the conflict. The Relief and Resettlement Commission shall co-ordinate activities and resources of the Organizations within the country.

Article 3. The first priority shall be the resettlement of displaced persons within the Sudan in the following order:
  (a) Persons presently residing in overcrowded centres in the Southern Region, and persons desirous to return to their original areas and homes;
  (b) Persons returning from the bush including Anya Nya Supporters;
  (c) Handicapped persons and orphans.

Article 4. The second priority shall be given to returnees from the neighbouring and other countries according to an agreed plan. This plan shall provide for:
  (a) Adequate reception centres with facilities for shelter, food supplies, medicine and medicaments;
  (b) Transportation to permanent resettlement villages or places of origin;
  (c) Materials and equipment.

Article 5. The Relief and Resettlement Commission shall:
  (a) Appeal to international organizations and voluntary agencies to continue assistance for students already under their support particularly for students in secondary schools and higher institutions until appropriate arrangements are made for their repatriation;
  (b) Compile adequate information on students and persons in need of financial support from the Sudan Government.

Article 6. The Relief and Resettlement Commission shall arrange for the education of all returnees who were attending primary schools.

This Agreement is hereby concluded on this twenty-seventh day of the month of February in the year one thousand nine hundred and seventy two, A.D., in this City, Addis Ababa, Ethiopia, between the Government of the Democratic Republic of the Sudan on the one hand and the Southern Sudan Liberation Movement on the other. It shall come into force on the date and hour fixed for its ratification by the President of the Democratic Republic of the Sudan and the Leader of the Southern Sudan Liberation Movement. It shall be ratified by the said two Leaders in person or through their respective authorised Representatives, in this City, Addis Ababa, Ethiopia, at the twelfth hour at noon, on the twelfth day of the month of March, in the year one thousand nine hundred and seventy two, A.D.

In witness whereof, We the Representatives of the Government of the Democratic Republic of the Sudan and the Representatives of the Southern Sudan Liberation Movement hereby append our signatures in the presence of the Representative of His Imperial Majesty the Emperor of Ethiopia and the Representatives of the World Council of Churches, the All Africa Conference of Churches, and the Sudan Council of Churches.

FOR THE GOVERNMENT OF THE DEMOCRATIC REPUBLIC OF THE SUDAN

1. Abel Alier-Wal Kuai, *Vice-President and Minister of State for Southern Affairs*
2. Dr. Mansour Khalid, *Minister for Foreign Affairs*
3. Dr. Gaafar Mohamed Ali Bakheit, *Minister for Local Government*
4. Major-General Mohamed Al Baghir Ahmed, *Minister of Interior*
5. Abdel Rahman Abdalla, *Minister of Public Service and Administrative Reform*
6. Brigadier Mirghani Suleiman
7. Colonel Kamal Abashar.

FOR THE SOUTHERN SUDAN LIBERATION MOVEMENT

1. Ezboni Mondiri Gwonza, *Leader of the Delegation*
2. Dr. Lawrence Wol Wol, *Secretary of the Delegation*

3. Mading deGarang, *Spokesman of the Delegation*
4. Colonel Frederick Brian Maggot, *Special Military Representative*
5. Oliver Batali Albino, *Member*
6. Angelo Voga Morjan, *Member*
7. Rev. Paul Puot, *Member*
8. Job Adier de Jok, *Member*

WITNESSES

1. Nabiyelul Kifle, *Representative of His Imperial Majesty, the Emperor of Ethiopia*
2. Leopoldo J. Niilus, *Representative of the World Council of Churches*
3. Kodwo E. Ankrah, *Representative of the World Council of Churches*
4. Burgess Carr, *General Secretary All Africa Conference of Churches*
5. Samuel Athi Bwogo, *Representative of Sudan Council of Churches*

ATTESTATION

I attest that these signatures are genuine and true

BURGESS CARR, *Moderator*

INDEX

Abas, Father Philip, 95
Abba, 64
Abbas Hamid Nasr, 14
Abboud, General Ibrahim,
   military regime, 1, 9, 48, 49,
   52, 73, 80
Abdalla Al Sayed, 14
Abdel Aziz Al Nasri, 3
Abdel Latif Al Khalifa, 14
Abdel Mageed Imam, 8
Abdel Nabi Abdel Gadir Mursal,
   32
Abdel Rahman Abdalla, 3, 14,
   107, 127, 176
Abdel Rahman Sule, 47
Abdulla Khalil, 48
Abiei, Gordon, 13, 53
Abu John, Samuel, 64
Acholi, 53
Action Committee for Africa —
   Biafra and Southern Sudan, 91
Action Medico, 91, 106
Addis Ababa, 91, 105, 126, 128,
   129, Israeli Embassy in, 41
Addis Ababa Agreement, 3, 66,
   107–20, 122, 123, 125, 129,
   133, 138, 143, 144, 152; and
   the language problem, 146; on
   the problem of South Sudan,
   158–77; and religion, 148;
   preparations for Conference,
   107
Adjang, Ferdinand, 52
Adwok, Luigi, 25, 31, 32, 49, 112
African Liberation Committee, 52
African Liberation Front, 54
African Unity, 7, 126, 135, 136,
   137
Africa Society, Frankfurt, 91
Agostini, Father, 94
Aguda, O., 134
Aguer, Nikanora, 13
Ahmed Morgan, 54
Akobo district, 61

Akol, Jacob, 101, 103
Akol, Peter, 14
Akot Ateim, 55, 64
Al Ayam, 3
Albino, Oliver, 51, 107, 127, 176;
   The Sudan — a Southern
   Viewpoint, 123
Al Fatih Abboud, 14
Algeria, 7, 89, 93
Al Hadi Al Mahdi's faction, 34
Ali Abdel Latif, 134
Ali Abu Sin, 101
Alier, Abel, 3, 14, 79, 83, 105,
   107, 119, 127; appointment as
   Vice-President and Minister of
   Southern Affairs, 99, 131, 176;
   appointment as President of
   the Provisional High Executive
   Council, 111, 115
Alier, Bullen, 48
Al Khatim Al Khalifa, Sir, 2;
   Government, 24
All Africa Conference of
   Churches, 104, 107, 129, 149,
   170, 176
Al Nasir, 38
Al Saraha, 73
Al Thawra, 108
Amadi district, 61
Amin, President, 109
Amin Nimir, 51
Amissah, S. H., 81
Amnesty Law, 73, 75, 76, 157
Amnesty provisions, 173
Amosa, Canon, 103
Anglican Church, 42
Angudri, 55, 68
Ankrah, Kodwo E., 81, 107, 128,
   177
Anti-Imperialist Front, 73, 79
Anti-Slavery Society, 89
Anya Nya: 4, 12, 15, 53, 57, 61,
   62, 63, 65, 100, 101, 103, 105;
   assistance from outside, 29;

attack by Army, 36; attacks on Sudanese Army posts, 95; Autonomy for the South, acceptance by the, 102; confrontation with Sudanese Army, 69, 85; committee for support of, 90; composition, 68; emblems, 93; hierarchy, 127; incorporation into Sudanese Army, 115, 116, 117–8, 119; increased activities, 27; military secessionist movement in, 140; negotiations between it and Sudan Government, 103; opposition to peace initiative, 106; organisation, 58; recognition by the Sudan Government, 104; relations between the S.A.N.U. and the, 52; representatives, 91; soldiers, 67; training, 58; training in Israel, 92; under Colonel Lagu's command, 66, 67

Anyidi Revolutionary Council, 64, 65

Anyidi State Government, 63, 64, 65

Anzara, 36, 76; events, 50

Arab Africa, 137

Arab-African unit, 137

Arab civilization, 88

Arabic, 33, 111, 145, 146, 147, 150, 159; pidgin, 54

Arab League, 41, 132, 134

Arab nationalism, 132, 135

Arab Socialists, 40

Arabs and world, 1, 89, 90, 96, 136, 137, 146, 151; Sudan relations with the, 132–35

Aru, Samuel, 14, 103, 105, 112

Arua, 94

Association of Southern Intellectuals, 130

Association for the Study of the World Refugee Problem, Norwegian section, 90

Atto, 64

Autonomy for the South, 102, 104

Aweil, district, 36, 38, 61; town, 36, 38

Ayik, Arop Yor, 29, 32

Ayol, Antipas, 61

Ayom, Gordon, 48

Azania Liberation Front (A.L.F.), 54, 55, 56

Babiker Awadalla, 8

Bahr el Ghazal province, 35, 38, 50, 51, 53, 61, 68, 110, 114, 116, 118, 159; defence committee, 61

Balgo-Bindi, 63

Barnard, Beverley, 91, 94

Basi, the, 63, 146

Batala, Major Paul Ali, 51, 64, 118

Bazia Renzi, 52

Beja, the, 146; area, 151

Beja Congress, 19, 30, 32, 34

Bentiu district, 61

Beshir, Darius, 3, 4

Biafra, 90, 93; Uli airstrip in, 90

Black Africa, 137

Bokassa, President, 109

Bol Madut, 36

'Bongo', 55

Bor area, 37, 38, 61

Border Commission, 29

Bouvert, Ruth, 91

Britain, 64, 116; colonies in Africa, 134

British, administration, 45, 142, 146; Members of Parliament, 82; trade unionists, 82; troops, 51

Bullingham, F., 93

Burjuk, Alfred, 48

Bwogo, Samuel Athi, 107, 128, 177

Cabral, Amilcar, 109

Cairo, 41, 109, 134

Cameroon, 6, 116

Caritas International, 91

Caritas (West Germany), 91, 106

Carr, Rev. Burgess, 104, 107, 128, 177

Carter, Roy, 82

Catholic Church, 42, 111, 145

Central African Republic, 40, 41, 64, 69, 83, 115; Government, 29, 41

Central Government Agencies, 163

Centralization, 140

Chad, 28, 83, 91, 137

Christian community, 147
Christianity, 33, 138, 147, 148, 149
Christian Science Monitor, 108
Christian South Sudanese guerillas, 92
Chueibet, 35; police post, 35, 36
Church organisations, 41, 95, 129
Church Relief Work, 91
Civil Service, 144
Clark, David, 82
Commission of Enquiry (1955), 147
Commission of the Churches on International Affairs, 100
Committee for Voluntary Organisations, Geneva, 83
Communist Party (C.P.), 14, 15, 21, 24, 25, 30, 40, 73, 74, 96; press, 29
Condominium administration, 143, 144, 146, 148, 149, 150; policy, 45
Congo, 5, 6, 7, 40, 53, 64, 91, 93, 95; Catholic Church organisations in the, 41; Kinshasa government, 41; rebels, 27; refugees, 41
Constituent Assembly, 32
Constitutional Assembly elections, 15
Constitutional Commission (1951), 74
Co-ordination Council, 78–79
Cotran Report, 49
Council of Ministers, 107
Council of Ministers Resolution N. III, 77–79
Coup d'états (November 1958), 156; (abortive, July 1971), 99, 124, 131
Cyprus, 116

Dada, Colonel David, 64
Dak, Othwan, 55, 142, 148
Daloka, 35
Dar es Salaam, 52
Darfur, 28; province, 30, 116, 151; languages, 146
Dawood Abdel Latif, 2, 3, 4
Dawn, 108
deGarang, Mading, 66, 82, 101, 102, 103, 104, 107, 112, 127, 176

Dei, Dak, 48
Democratic Unionist Party, 34
Deffarge, Claude, 92
Deng, Elia, 55
Deng, Santino, 9, 14, 26, 51, 53
Deng, Solomon, 55
Deng, William, 2, 4, 8, 9, 14, 26, 29, 31, 32; in exile, 52; murder, 38; return to the Sudan, 53
Dinka, the, 50, 63, 112, 142, 147; dominance in the Nile Government, 65; language, 146, 147
Diori, President, 28
Diu, Buth, 9, 26, 29, 31, 32, 46, 47, 48, 53, 105
Diu, Nyang, 51
Divall, Anthony, 91
Dubai, 116

East Africa, 129, 136; goodwill visits to, 28, 99
East African Common Market, 61
East Germany, 89
Economic and Planning Committee for the South, 78–9
Education, 144–5
Edwards, Robert, 82
Egypt, 7, 41, 42, 87, 88, 89, 90, 116, 131, 134, 135, 136; Government, 109; nationalists, 132
Eliaba Sunur, 64
English (language), 33, 111, 146, 147, 159
Entebbe, 94, 95
Equatoria defence committee, 61
Equatoria Corps, 50; mutiny, 49
Equatoria province, 35, 36, 37, 38, 51, 61, 68, 110, 114, 118; Central, 61; East, 50, 61; West, 50, 55
Eritrean Liberation Front, 29
Eritrean rebels, 29, 40; refugees, 29
Erkawit Conference, 88
Ethiopia, 6, 7, 28, 40, 64, 69, 83, 91, 95, 115, 116, 126; agreement between the Sudan and, 83–5; relations with the Sudan, 28–9, 40, 41, 135, 136; Sudan Ambassador in, 104

Euor, Capt. Emanuel, 64
Europe, 91, 99, 123; Southern representatives in, 100

Fanjak, 61
Fashala, 28, 38
Fashoda National Provisional Government, 54
Faustino Roro, 46
Federal Block, 49
Federalism, 139
Ferrari, Father, 69, 124
Feruge tribe, 46
Five-Year Development Plan, 87
Foot, Sir Dingle, 129
Free Southern Front (F.S.F.), 9, 30, 31, 53
French Army, 93
Fung region, 151
Fur, the, 146
Fürstenberg, Eliman, 91

Gaafar Mohamed Ali Bakheit, Dr., 107, 176
Gabeit Infantry School, 119
Gabon, 93, 116
Gabrial Kao, 55
Gamaa Hassan, 112
Gambaila, 41, 69
Garang, Franco, 103
Garang, Joseph, 9, 53, 73, 74, 101, 103
Gbeng, Christopher, 53
Geneva, 126, 129
Germany, East, 89
Germany, West, 94, 95
Gezira, 150
Ghana, 6, 7, 128, 135
Ghoremia Village, 35
Goode, Izbon, 61
Gor, the, 63
Graduates Congress, 45, 46
Grass Curtain, The, 82, 90, 101, 103, 127
Gypkens, Franz, 91

Haile Selassie, Emperor, 40, 107, 109, 126, 128, 176
Haq, Barbara, 82, 101, 103, 120n
Hassan Ahmed Yousif, 3
Hassan Al Turabi, Dr., 14
Hassan, Cleto, 103, 105

High Executive Council, 110; Interim, 170–1, 174; President, 110, 159, 162, 163, 164
Holmes, Joe, 82
'Home guards', 37–38, 39
Howell, John, 48
Iba, 35
Ibo (Nigeria), 141
Idali, 64
Indemnity Act (1967), 42
India, 134
Indochina, 93
Independents' party, 31
International Peace Movement, 61
International Red Cross, 89, 170
Islam, 33, 91, 134, 138, 146–9
Islam and Sharia law, 33
Islamic Africa, 137
Islamic Charter Front (I.C.F.), 14, 17, 29, 30, 33, 34
Islamic Constitution, 34, 124
Islamic Law, 138, 148
Islamic Socialist Party, 30
Islamization, 149
Ismail al Azhari, 48
Ismail Salim, 50
Israel, 42, 68, 69, 95, 135, 136; involvement in the Southern problem, 91–2, 95, 124, 152
Italy, 64, 93, 116

Jaden, Aggrey, 8, 9, 52, 54, 55, 56, 61, 63, 64, 124
Jamal Abdel Nasser, 135
Jamus, Honga, 36
Jean, Capt. Sunday, 64
Job Adier de Jok, 107, 177
Joint-Commission, 170
Joint Military Commission, 68, 118, 119, 172, 173
Juba, 4, 6, 27, 35, 36, 37, 38, 47, 50, 51, 104, 170, 173, 174; as capital of Southern Region, 166; Conference on repatriation and resettlement of refugees (1972), 116; Erkawit Conference in, 88; Graduates Congress Committees in, 46; growth of population in, 76; Medical Assistant School re-opening in, 80; Provincial Council in, 80–1; state of emergency, 5; Youth Festival, 82

Juba Conference (1947), 11, 24, 26, 30, 46 -7, 110
Jume, Daniel, 49, 50, 61
June Declaration *see* Nimeiri
Jur River region, 61

Kabish, 64
Kajo-Kaji, 53, 94
Kamal Abashar, Colonel, 107, 127, 176
Kampala, 4, 52, 91, 93, 94; Kampala, Bishop of, 94
Kangi station, 37
Kao, Ibrahim, 54
Kaplan, Gunter, 91
Kapoeta, 38, 50, 61, 68, 76
Kassala province, 30, 116
Katire, 53
Kaunda, President, 109
Kaya, 53
Kayl, Harry, 82
Kenya, 7, 95, 136; Government, 28, 29
Kenyiba airstrip, 94
Khamis, Dr. Clement, 54
Khartoum, 6, 85, 95, 96, 104, 105, 126, 150; authorities, 51; Church representatives' visit to, 129; conference on relief and resettlement in, 106; December 1964 events in, 4; Governments, 67, 79, 100, 116, 124; High Court of Appeals in, 27; province, 116; University, 8; World Council of Churches/All Africa Conference of Churches mission to, 100
Khartoum North, 150
Khor Englizi, 37
Kitchener, 147
Kitgum, 39
Kodok district, 38, 61
Koranic schools, 46
Korea, 93
Kordofan province, 30, 116, 151
Kujurs, 48
Kur area, 37
Kuwait, 89
Kwak, David, 55
Kwanai, George, 55, 61
Kwanji, Arkangel, 55
Kwat, Camelio Dhol, 55, 58, 63, 64
Kwot, Daniel, 55

Ladjor, Lazo, 55
Lagu, Colonel Joseph, 64, 66, 67, 95, 100, 101, 102, 103, 104, 118, 127, 131
Lam, Stephen, 55
Language, 145—46
Lasu, 53
Latuka, 53
Legislative Assembly, 47, 75
Leopodville, 52
Lernyo village, 35
Lestor, Joan, British M.P., 82
Liberal Party, 31, 47, 48, 49, 50
Liberia, 128, 135
Libya, 87, 88, 89
Logali, Hilary Paul, 14, 34, 47, 53, 103, 105, 112
Lohure, Fr. Saturnino, 39, 52, 53
London, 82, 90, 101, 103; Sudan Embassy in, 101
Lubi, Samuel, 105
Lubiri secondary school, Uganda, 94
Luili, 50
Luking, 39
Lupai, Samuel, 112
Lupe, Elia, 49, 54, 55, 64, 112
Lwat, Andolf, 55
Lwoke, Benjamin, 47, 48

MacDermot, B.H.D., 82, 103
Madagascar, 93
Madi, language, 53; witches, 53
Maduot, Tobi, 112
Maggot, Colonel Frederick B., 64, 89, 107, 127, 176
Mahjoub Mohamed Salih, 3, 28, 29, 34; Government, 16, 26, 34
Majok, Philemon, 9, 26, 34
Makerere University, 91; Students' Guild at, 80
Malakal, 4, 46, 50, 104, 174; district, 61; Provincial Council in, 80
Mali, 137
Malut Scheme, 142
Malwal, Bona, 13, 14, 112
Malwal, Joshua, 14, 33
Mansour Khalid, Dr., 176
Mauritania, 138
Mayer, Francis, 55
May Revolution, 132

May Revolutionary Government, 72
Mazrui, Ali, 137, 138
Mbali, Alexis, 52
Mboro, Clement, 24, 34, 53, 104, 112, 115
Mboro police post, 35
McCall, S., 53, 91
McClore, 69
McLoughlin, Peter, 150
Medical Assistant School, 81
Mercenaries, 91, 93, 95
Meridi, 4, 37, 38, 61, 76
Middle East, 136, 151
Military College, 80
Minister for Southern Affairs, 75, 77, 78, 79, 83, 99, 101, 105, 107
Ministry of Education, setting-up of a department for Christian Affairs in, 81
Ministry of Interior, 4
Ministry of Southern Affairs, 74, 75, 86, 96
Ministry of Works Labour Camps, 35
Mirghani Suleiman, Brigadier, 107, 127, 176
Missionaries, 41, 106, 124, 144, 149, 152
Missionary Act (1962), 42
Missionary societies, 144, 146, 149
Mobis, Simon, 55
Mobutu, President, 109
Mohamed Ahmed Mahjoub, 15, 26, 32; coalition Government, 72
Mohamed Ahmed Mardi, 13
Mohamed Al Baghir Ahmed, Major-General, 105, 107, 176
Mohamed, Amedo Awad, 55, 64
Mohamed Dawood Al Khalifa, 14
Mohamed/Ibrahim Abu Salim, 3
Mohamed Ibrahim Nugud, 14
Mohamed Salih Al Shingeiti, 30
Mondiri, Ezboni, 24, 49, 54, 55, 63, 107, 112, 127, 176
Morning Post, 108
Morocco, 116
Mortu, 64, 94, 95
Moru language, 53
Movement for Colonial Freedom (M.C.F.), 82, 83, 101, 102, 104

Mozi, Clement, 55
Mudathir Abdel Ralim, 3
Mundiri area, 68
Muortat Mayen, Gordon, 53, 55, 63, 64, 124
Musa Shol, 105
Muslim Brothers, 24, 40, 124; press, 29
Muslim Community, 81, 147

Nabiyelul Kifle, 107, 128, 177
Nairobi, 91
Nasir district, 61
National Armed Forces, 169; N.C.O.s in, 50, 51, 118, 119; officers in, 118; privates in, 118
National Constitution Commission, 31, 32, 33, 34, 38
National Constitution Conference; Technical Committee, 32
National Plan, 111
National Unionist Party (N.U.P.), 14, 17, 24, 26, 29, 31, 33, 48
New York, 103
New York Times, 108
Niger, 28, 137
Nigeria, 7, 54, 137, 141
Niilus, Leopold J., 107
Nile Basin region, 61
Nile Mirror, 144
Nile Provincial Government (N.P.G.), 63, 65, 66
Nile Valley, unity of the, 134
Nile Unity Party, 34
Nilo-Hamitic languages, 146
Nilotic group of languages, 146
Nilotics, the, 141
Nimeiri, President Gaafar Mohamed, 72, 83, 85, 107, 127, 130; policy statement on Southern Question (June 1969), 76, 86, 87, 88, 96, 105, 110, 122, 131, 151, 155–7, 158; statement in Cairo (1970), 87; visit to Ethiopia, 84
Nimule, 35, 53
Nkrumah, Kwame, 135
Non-Arab Africa, 137
Non-black Africa, 137
Non-Islamic Africa, 137

Northern Sudan, 26, 41, 124, 134, 136, 142, 149; identification with Egypt, 136; six provinces, 18
Norway, 90
Norwegian Association for the Southern Sudan, 90
Nuba, the, 146
Nuba Mountain region, 95, 151
Nuba Mountains Association, 19, 30, 32, 34
Nubian (language), 146
Nuer, the, 50, 63, 142, 146
Nygory, Colonel Paul, 64

Obang, Philip, 3
Obote, President, 39, 83, 95
Observer, The, 108
Ochala, Hilary, 13
Ocheng, Pancrasio, 52, 61
Odimiang, Benjamin, 50
Oduhu, Joseph, 8, 9, 49, 52, 54, 55, 64, 112
Ojukwu, General, 93
Omdurman, 108, 150
Olwak, Natale, 13, 85, 103, 105
Onama, F. K., 9
Opari district, 53
Opul, Massio, 61
Oregat, Valeridio, 52
Organization of African Unity (O.A.U.), 6, 7, 28, 52, 106, 108, 126, 132, 133; Commission for Refugees, 6, 52; contribution to relief programme, 116; involvement of Sudan in activities, 152; Liberation Committee funds, 85; meetings of Heads of State, 85; observer team, 104
Oslo, Bishop of, 90
Osman Sid Ahmed Ismail, 3
Owing Kibul, 64, 66, 95
Oyet, Nathaniel, 52

Pachola, 53
Palestine problem, 132
Pan-Africanism, 7, 135, 136, 137, 151
Pan-Africanist movement, 135
Pan-Arabism, 137, 151
Pango station, 37
Paul VI, Pope, 83
Pauli, Michael, 64

Paysama, Stanislaus, 47, 48, 49
'Peace Movement', 62
Pedak, Philip, 52, 54
Pedit, Tadio, 55
People's Armed Forces, 165, 172
People's Democratic Party (P.D.P.), 14, 15, 21, 25, 30, 35, 40
People's National Assembly, 159, 162, 163
People's Regional Assembly, 111, 113, 159–66, 168, 171, 172
Police College, 80
Political Parties' Conference, 29, 30, 31, 32, 34, 38, 110, 128
Popular revolution of October 21, 155, 156
Portugal, 93
Preston, John, 82
Professional Front, 14
Protocol on Interim Arrangements, 165
Provisional Order No. 40, 111, 113, 115
Provisional High Executive Council, 111, 113, 114
Puot, Rev. Paul, 64, 107, 127, 177

Qatar, 116

Rabat, 109
Ramba, Lubari, 14, 16
Reed, Allan, 69
Regional assembly, 111; elections for the, 114, 115
Regional autonomy, 73; programme, 156–7
Regional, Civil Service, 171; Council, 32; Executive Council, 163, 165, 166; High Executive Council, 117
Regionalism, 140–1
Regional, Legislation, 160, 166; Public Service, 111, 164; Self-Government Act, 107, 110, 111, 115, 117, 139
Rehfisch, Farnham, 150
Renk district, 38, 61
Repatriation Commission, 173–4
Republican Party, 30
Resettlement and Rehabilitation Commission, 112, 174

Revolt of the Equatoria Corps, 67
Revolutionary Council, 72, 75, 87
Revolution of May 25, 155, 156, 158
Revolution of October 1964, 8, 9, 72
Rhodesia, 93
Ring, Andrew, W., 14
Robinson, David, 91, 92
Rome, 83, 90
Round Table Conference, 1–13, 22, 25, 26, 38, 63, 72, 110, 122; Arabs' role in the, 1; implementation of resolutions of the, 15, 16; objectives, 125; Rules of Procedure, 11; reconvening, 21, 30–1; resolutions, 17, 128; secretariat, 3, 127; 'Special Minute', 12–13, 17
Rumbek, 35, 38, 51; district, 61
Rume, Marko, 50, 52, 54, 55

Sadig El Mahdi, 17, 29; Government, 31, 32
Safarino Foly, 55
Samuel, Rudolph I., 141
Saturlino, 50, 51
Saudi Arabia, 116
Scandinavian countries, 83, 90
Security Council, 6
Senegal, 137
Shakeri hills, 37
Sharia, 33
Shilluk, the, 146
Signals and Engineering divisions, 50
Six-Day War, 92, 93
Siyad Barre, President, 109
Sobat Valley region, 61
Socialism, 151
Socialists Democratic Group, 15
Somalia, 116, 137
South and Nuba Mountains Association, 33
South Africa, 93
'Southern Air-Motive', 91
Southern Command, 119
Southern Corps, 118
Southerners, mutiny (1955), 24; national loyalty, 142
Southern Front, 9, 10, 13, 14, 17, 24, 25, 26, 30, 32, 53, 87; activists, 112; activities, 5; and the appointment of regional governors, 31; on educational policy, 20; elections results, 34; letter to President Obote, 39; members' hostility to North, 27; as part of coalition, 34; S.S.P.G. condemnation of, 62; and Sudan Constitution, 33
Southernization, 11, 16
Southern National Peace Party, 31
Southern Officials' Welfare Committee, 46
Southern Party, 47, *see also* Liberal Party
Southern policy, 45
Southern political leaders, 12, 126; activities against the Sudan, 40; large meeting outside the Sudan, 55
Southern Provinces Regional Self-Government Act, 120, 151
Southern refugees, 126
Southern Region, 159–66, 168, 172, 174; agreement on the cease-fire in the, 169–70
Southern Sudan, 34–5, 37, 41, 42, 90; the Africans in the, 134–5; Autonomous, 86; citizenship for the, 110; disagreements between the civil and military authorities in the, 50; draft act on regional self-government for the, 105; economic gap between North and, 142, 143; elections (1958) in the, 49; employment of African priests and churchmen in, 42; identification with East Africa, 136; international policies in, 92; liberation from Arab rule under S.S.P.G. Constitution, 56; national unity under S.S.P.G. programme, 56; politics, 48; promotion of economic and social development in the, 120; regional self-government for the, 151, 152; resolution of the U.N. Association of New York on, 89; security situation, 15; status, 1; three provinces, 4, 18, 60–1, 158, 159
Southern Sudan Association in London, 82, 90, 101

Southern Sudan Intellectuals Association, 87
Southern Sudan Liberation Front, 88
Southern Sudan Liberation Movement (S.S.L.M.), 66, 127, 169, 170, 175–6
Southern Sudan Provisional Government (S.S.P.G.), 55; foreign policy, 61; functions and duties of the different ministries in the, 58–60, 62; programme, 56–8
Southern Sudan Social and Political Association, 46
Southern Youth and Students Organisations, 87
Soviet Union, the, 89, 90, 96
Special Commission for Relief and Resettlement, 174, 175
Special Tribunal, 173
Stanley-Baker, Judge R. C., 75
Steiner, Rolf, 93, 95; statement to the Uganda Government, 93–5; trial, 95
Stern, Jack, 82
Sudan, Democratic Republic of the, 86, 105, 159, 166, 175; activities against the, 40; Arabism and Africanism, 133–5; British-controlled schools in the, 134; Central Government, 40, 41, 82, 99, 101, 102, 128, 129, 143, 144, 168; division into nine regions, 30–1; education in the, 144, 145; Egypt's close associations with the, 7; independence, 48, 135; as member of the Commission for Refugees, 6; multiple marginality, 137; parliament, 39; peace in the, 122; Permanent Constitution (May 1973), 138, 148, 149, 150; President, 170, 176; regional self-government for the, 141, 145, 158; relations with Ethiopia, 28–9; role in Afro-Arab relations, 88; support for the Palestinian cause, 42; unity, 103, 104, 120, 122, 139
Sudan Administrative Conference, 47

Sudan African Closed Districts National Union (S.A.C.D.N.U.), 52
Sudan African Freedom Fighters, 54
Sudan African National Union (S.A.N.U.), 2, 5, 6, 7, 9, 13, 14, 17, 25, 26, 29, 30, 31, 33, 53, 87; appeals to call off fighting, 4, 5; divisions, 34; faction, 32; leaders in Kampala, 14; members, 27; place in elections, 34; S.S.P.G. condemnation of, 62; supporters outside the Sudan, 52, 54
Sudan African Socialist Union, 53
Sudan Azania organisation, 63
Sudan Constitution, new, 120
Sudan Council of Churches, 107, 128–29, 176
Sudanese Army, 40, 95, 129; incorporation of the Anya Nya in, 115, 116, 117
Sudanese Nationalists, 132
Sudanese Nationalist Act (1957), 159
Sudanese rebels, 40, 41, 105, 106, 129, 131
Sudanese refugees, 7, 40, 41, 42, 83, 89, 91, 92, 106, 115, 136; resettlement, 115, 119; settlements, 69
Sudan Gazette, 104
Sudanic languages, 146
Sudanization policy, 49
Sudan Liberation Movement, 107
Sudan Socialist Union, 151, 170; Political Bureau, 107; preparatory committee, 105, 131
Sudan Unity Party (S.U.P.), 9, 10, 14, 26, 30, 31, 53
Suez, 93
Sunday Nation, 108
Sunday Times, 90, 92
Supreme Council, 25, 26
Supreme Court, 26
Suru, Capt. Hybok, 64
Syria, 29

Taffeng, Major-General, 51, 63, 64, 65, 66, 94, 95, 118
Tali, 35

Tanzania, 6, 7, 54, 116; Government, 28; Ministry of Foreign Affairs, 109
Taweel, Michael, 112
Tekaka, 35
Third World revolutionaries, 41
Tombalbaye, President, 28, 109
Tombura, 36, 76
Tonj, 35, 38; district, 61
Torit, 50, 76, 92; district, 38, 61, 68; event, 50
Toynbee, Arnold, 123
Treaty of Versailles, 122
Trench, Terry, 82
Tripoli Agreement, 87
Troller, Gordian, 92
Tshombe, M., 6
Tumbura, 38
Twelve-Man Committee, 3, 13, 15, 17, 20, 25, 29, 33, 38, 110, 127; achievements, 21; final report, 18, 30, 32; on the issue of financial and economic relations, 20; meetings, 21–2; recommendations, 128

Uganda, 64, 103, 132, 136; Abel Alier's visit to, 79; Church groups in, 40; Government, 6, 28, 29, 93; Israeli Embassy in, 91; Israeli presence in, 92; member of Commission for Refugees, 6; observer at Round Table Conference, 7; Steiner's visit to, 94–5; Sudanese refugees in, 38, 39, 69, 115; trade agreement with, 83
Umma Party, 14, 17, 24, 26, 30, 31, 33, 34, 48; divisions in, 34
United Nations (U.N.), the, 7, 55, 88; Commission of Human Rights, 89, 90; General Assembly, 83, 103, 109; High Commissioner for Refugees, 69, 116, 170, 174; special agencies, 106
United States of America, 64, 116; Embassy, 6
United Day, 108
United Party, 31
University of Khartoum, School of Extra-Mural Studies, 83
Upper Nile Defence Committee, 61

Upper Nile Political Association, 46
Upper Nile Province, 36, 37, 38, 41, 50, 51, 61, 68, 110, 114, 118, 159; Governor, 49

Vatican, the, 83
Verona Fathers, 91, 94
Vigilant, 34
Vocational training centres, 81
Voga Morjan, Angelo, 107, 177
Voice of the People, 108
Voice of the Southern Sudan, 90, 127

Wai, Dunstan, M., 65, 66
Wani, Arkangelo, 64
Wani, Gabriel, 64
Wani, L., 54
Wani, Serafino Swaka, 94
Wau, 4, 36, 37, 46, 50, 51, 53, 104, 174; extension of the railway to, 142; fruit canning factory, 142; incidents, 27; Hospital, 35; Provincial Council in, 80
Wek Achian, James, 52
West African languages, 146
Western domination, 132
West Germany, 39, 64, 95
White League Society, 134
Wieu, Andrew, 13, 26, 105
Wol, Alfred, 26, 32
Wol, Ambrose, 14
Wol Wol, Lawrence, 55, 61, 66, 89, 101, 102, 107, 112, 127, 176
Working Forces of the People, 114
World Council of Churches, 81–3, 104, 107, 149, 170, 176; representatives, 128, 129, 131; study of Israeli involvement in Southern problem, 91–2
World Council of Churches/All African Conference Churches mission, 99–100

Yak, Andrew, 55
Yak, Jervase, 29
Yak, Solomon, 61
Yambio, 36, 38, 50, 76; district, 61, 68
Yassin Omer El Imam, 14

Yei, 50, 76; district, 61
Yei River area, 68
Yez, 46
Yirol, 37
Yousif Mohamed Ali, 3, 13, 14
Yugoslavia, 116

Zaire, 69, 83, 91, 115, 136
Zande, the, 142, 146
Zande Scheme, 142